Cultural Writings of Franz Rosenzweig

Library of Jewish Philosophy

Cultural Writings of Franz Rosenzweig

Edited and translated from the German by
Barbara E. Galli

With a Foreword by
Leora Batnitzky

Syracuse University Press

Library of Congress Cataloging-in-Publication Data

Rosenzweig, Franz, 1886–1929.
Cultural writings of Franz Rosenzweig / edited and translated from the German
by Barbara E. Galli with a foreword by Leora Batnitzky.
p. cm.—(Library of Jewish philosophy)
Includes bibliographical references (p.) and index.
ISBN 0-8156-2833-1 (cloth : alk. paper)—ISBN 0-8156-2834-X
(pbk. : alk. paper)
1. Rosenzweig, Franz, 1886–1929. 2. Judaism—Germany. 3. Musical
criticism. 4. Rosenzweig, Franz, 1886–1929—Contributions in musical
criticism. I. Galli, Barbara E.
(Barbara Ellen), 1949– II. Title. III. Series.
BM755.R6 A5 2000
296.3′092—dc21   99-088989

For, the heavens are telling,
my music making friends,
Anna and Horace Rosenberg

Barbara E. Galli is with McGill University's Faculty of Religious Studies. She is author of *Franz Rosenzweig and Jehuda Halevi: Translating, Translations, and Translators* as well as numerous articles on Rosenzweig's thought. She is co-editor (with Alan Udoff) of *Franz Rosenzweig's "The New Thinking"* and editor of *God, Man, and the World: Lectures and Essays* (also published by Syracuse University Press).

Contents

Foreword

LEORA BATNITZKY

The essays collected in *Cultural Writings of Franz Rosenzweig* offer the English reader a glimpse into the cultural and social dimensions of Rosenzweig's thought. This aspect of his thought has too often been ignored because of an over-emphasis on Rosenzweig's status as a "religious thinker"—a category he explicitly rejects—and particularly on his arguments about revelation. The essays translated here provide a broader context than this status might suggest through which to understand some of the most central concerns of Rosenzweig's thought, as well as the source of those concerns: Rosenzweig's conception of the crisis of meaning in the modern world. Rosenzweig's views of Judaism and the possibilities of revelation for the modern person are intimately connected with these broad concerns but the former

Parts of this essay are taken from Leora Batnitzky, *Idolatry and Representation: The Philosophy of Franz Rosenzweig Reconsidered* (Princeton University Press, 2000).

cannot be understood outside of the context of the latter. In my brief preface to Barbara Galli's wonderful translation of Rosenzweig's cultural writings, I would like to outline briefly why this is the case. Indeed, I will suggest that neglecting the intimate connection between Rosenzweig's views of the importance of tradition in the modern world and the possibility of revelation for the modern person can only distort Rosenzweig's corpus.

Rosenzweig's philosophy is usually described as existentialist, neo-Hegelian, or, as has been advocated most recently, postmodern.[1] But as I have suggested elsewhere, it is perhaps more helpful to think of Rosenzweig in the philosophical context of contemporary tradition-oriented thinkers, such as Alasdair MacIntyre in the Anglo-American context, and Hans-Georg Gadamer in the Continental one.[2] The essays translated in this collection show us the inherent limitations of the existentialist, neo-Hegelian, and postmodern interpretations of Rosenzweig. Recognizing the complex, multi-layered relations between Rosenzweig's approaches to Judaism and to philosophy allows us to see the ways in which his early-twentieth-century musings on the nature of religious tradition and the possibility of the modern authority of these musings both anticipate and go beyond current arguments by contemporary tradition-oriented thinkers.

Reference to Rosenzweig's supplementary essay to *The Star of Redemption*, "The New Thinking," recently translated and published by Barbara Galli and Alan Udoff, is helpful here. Rosenzweig describes his theory of knowledge as a "messianic theory of knowledge, which evaluates truths according to the price of its verification and to the bond that they establish among human beings."[3] He explains his understanding of verification in the following way: "From those least important truths, of the type 'two times two is four,' on which people easily agree, without using up more than a little brain grease—for the multiplication table something else, for the theory of relativity a little more—the path leads over the truths that have cost man something on toward those that he cannot verify except with the sacrifice of his life, and finally to those whose truth can be verified only by the commitment of the lives of all generations. . . ."[4] Here we can begin to appreciate Rosenzweig's hermeneutic sensibilities. He maintains that the crisis of meaning in the modern world is a crisis of losing our most basic hermeneutic orientation. Rosenzweig argues that the epistemological and existential crises of the twentieth century converge in our inability to understand how human meaning is constituted, sustained, and reinvented. The "new thinking" seeks to restore to the modern person this possibility of fundamental orientation.

In this important sense, Rosenzweig's thought anticipates and challenges the thought of Hans Georg Gadamer, who defines hermeneutics and the problem of hermeneutics for the modern person in the following way: "It is not so much our judgments as it is our prejudices that constitute our being. . . . [T]he historicity of our existence entails that prejudices, in the literal sense of the word, constitute the initial directedness of our whole ability to experience. Prejudices are biases of our openness to the world. They are simply conditions whereby we experience something—whereby what we encounter says something to us."[5] Like Rosenzweig before him, Gadamer contends that the inability to recognize the ways in which our identities are constituted by indebtedness to the past has produced a crisis of meaning in the modern world. Gadamer maintains that the way out of this crisis is to return to a pre-Enlightenment understanding of prejudice, not as a biased distortion of truth, but as a precondition of the possibility of truth. Literally, a prejudice is a prejudgment (*Vorurteil*). Prejudices make judgments possible. They are the underlying bases of our identities that allow us to be critical.

As we saw earlier in the quotation from "The New Thinking," Rosenzweig makes a similar point when he argues, not against scientific or mathematical truth, but rather for the priority of those most important truths that are verified by the lives that are risked and often lost to honor them. Rosenzweig would thus push Gadamer further, although this difference between them is more a matter of emphasis than of substance. Rosenzweig's position makes clear the price of taking the past seriously in the present. The price, Rosenzweig maintains, is life itself. In contrast, Gadamer's position on the present's indebtedness to the past often sounds overly cognitive.[6] Moreover, Gadamer's analysis might imply that prejudices, or prejudgments, are more passive than they actually are. Whereas Rosenzweig would agree with Gadamer in criticizing a purely cognitive approach to identity—Rosenzweig and Gadamer would agree that a prejudgment (*Vorurteil*) precedes a judgment (*Urteil*)—Rosenzweig would argue that prejudices are also full of risks and are quite costly both to individuals and to communities.

There is another important difference in emphasis between Rosenzweig and Gadamer. Where Gadamer presents *Truth and Method* as a general theory of hermeneutics, Rosenzweig's *Star of Redemption* is more particular than a generic hermeneutic. Rosenzweig's hermeneutical approach is also an attempt to negotiate Judaism's relation to modern thought. However, the particularity of Rosenzweig's approach is in keeping with his general hermeneutical argument. Rather than reflecting a parochial point of view, Rosenzweig's position may be more compelling than Gadamer's, at least on *hermeneutical* grounds. Where Gadamer appears to be satisfied with locating the generic fact that our judgments are always constituted by particular prejudices, he does not indicate *the cost* of his particular prejudices. He does not explore the truths for which his ancestors have died and upon which his own prejudices are based. Rosenzweig goes further and situates his particular prejudices. Rosenzweig claims that it is possible to see the universality of the hermeneutical problem only from a particular position, that is, as a situated person.

We are now in a position to turn to the essays translated here. Again and again in these essays, Rosenzweig maintains that the possibility of universality is "now" only open from the vantage point of particularity. It is essential to recognize that Rosenzweig does not give up on the possibility of universality but only on the pretension that the particular is either inconsequential or inherently dangerous. Suggesting in his essay "Hic et Ubique!" ("Here and Everywhere!") that "everywhere" is made possible only by way of one's "here," Rosenzweig argues that the crisis of capitalism brings with it a crisis of the book industry. Both crises share an essential characteristic, which is a failure to recognize the embodied particularity of individuals:

> In the end the book does not possess any magical powers that could compel the harmless passerby to become a reader. No book opens itself; he who opens it and leafs through it after all has to attribute this to himself. So if this ocean was not intended to be emptied, then perhaps to be swum through. It was probably enough if these books only found owners instead of readers. And really, the great magician capitalism brought this about: it was obviously able to force for its products if not readers, then buyers.

A capitalist, consumer-oriented society defines both reading and readers generically, implying that books read themselves by faceless readers. Against this assumption Rosenzweig argues that "time asks the human beings of today nothing less than: Who are you? who do you want to be? you as whole human being, not in one part of your being, and in being so asked, he senses how already the answer to these questions lies prepared which had only remained mute till now because no one asked the question."

Rosenzweig proposes that books again be "written for particular bodies." The impetus for his argument is not a kind of parochialism but a "counterbalance" to an over-emphasis on the generic spirit as opposed to the particular body. Rosenzweig argues here in a less detailed and technical fashion than he does in *The Star of Redemption* that there are ideally three types of people. "Today one after the other is beginning to discover who he is: Christian, Jew, pagan speak their loud and decisive: 'This is what I am,' which had not been heard for a long time." Rosenzweig suggests three reconstructed publishing houses: a Christian, a pagan, and a Jewish one. In this way, "embodied spiritual [*geistig*] communities" will stand facing the writer and reader alike.

One might find Rosenzweig's proposal for separate Jewish, Christian, and pagan publishing houses jarring in the context of his somewhat well-known comment in "The New Thinking" that *The Star of Redemption* is not "a Jewish book."[7] There Rosenzweig claims that although the *Star* discusses Judaism, it does so no more comprehensively than it does Christianity and Islam. The book should rather be seen as a system of philosophy. Here we have an opportunity to encounter the rich complexity of Rosenzweig's argument about the relation between "here" and "everywhere." Although the *Star* is not "a Jewish book," it is written from the particular position of a Jewish writer. From Rosenzweig's perspective, a Jewish writer does not make a book Jewish. Rather, such an embodied writer endows his work with the possibility of speaking in a voice that can be authoritative equally from the perspective of the future as well as from that of the past. He writes:

But the "Jewish book"? as the very title seems to indicate? . . . I received the new thinking in these old words, thus I have rendered it and passed it on, in them. I know that to a Christian, instead of mine, the words of the New Testament would have come to his lips; to a pagan, I think, although not words of his holy books—for their ascent leads away from the original language of mankind, not toward it like the earthly path of revelation—but perhaps entirely his own words. But, to me, these words. And yet this is a Jewish

book: not one which deals with "Jewish matters," for then
the books of the Protestant Old Testament would be Jewish
books, but one for which the old Jewish words come in
order to say what it has to say, and precisely for the new
things it has to say. Jewish matters are, as matters generally
are, always already past; but Jewish words, even if old, take
part in the eternal youth of the word, and the word is
opened to them, then they will renew the word.[8]

With the above qualifications, Rosenzweig argues that
The Star of Redemption is "a Jewish book" in the sense, not
that it concerns Jewish matters, but that it is animated by
Jewish words. Jewish words, however, are not to be mistaken for a comprehensive view of or statement from "Judaism."[9] In the *Star*, Jewish words allow for a particular
articulation of the "new thinking," one that has universal
implications. Rosenzweig's philosophy of language is one of
call and response, which he describes succinctly in the *Star*
as follows: "For the word is mere inception until it finds
reception in an ear, and response in a mouth (*das Wort ist
bloß ein Anfang, bis es auf das Ohr trifft, das es auf- fängt, und
auf den Mund, der ihm ant-wortet*)."[10] It is important to note
Rosenzweig's use of sound as the principal description of his
philosophy of language. For Rosenzweig, hearing and re-
sponding are among the "Jewish" elements of his Jewish
words. Note the contrast to Gadamer, who leaves un-
acknowledged the *existential* (though not historical) import
of his use of vision and seeing to describe the universality of
the hermeneutic situation: "The horizon is the range of vision that includes everything that can be seen from a particular vantage point."[11] Intrinsic to Rosenzweig's "new

thinking" is the recognition that the universal can only come by way of the particular; "everywhere" is reached only from "here."

Also intrinsic to the "new thinking" is the notion that Jewish or other "matters" turn a living tradition into objects and indeed into fossils of the past. If a tradition is to have a future, Rosenzweig argues that it must turn matters of the past into words of the present and future. It is in this context that I suggest the reader approach Rosenzweig's essays on the significance of Moses Mendelssohn and of G. E. Lessing's "Nathan the Wise," which are translated for the first time in this volume. In criticizing the legacy of Mendelssohn and Lessing's universalism (and not so much Mendlessohn himself), Rosenzweig proposes a "new solution to the problem of tolerance," one that moves away from viewing particularity as generic or incidental. We read in Rosenzweig's essay "Lessing's Nathan": "And that is now the new solution to the problem of tolerance: 'Only because you are Edom may I be Yaakov.' No more the coexistence of two statues, no longer the indifferent confusion that one tried earlier to read out of Nathan the Wise, no: organic coherence, organic beside—, against—and with-one-another (only the particular case can teach which of these three) of Jewish and Christian human beings." Mendelssohn, Rosenzweig maintains, left German Jews "defenseless" in his quest for a generic universalism that rendered the German-Jewish relation impossible. As Rosenzweig reiterates in a number of contexts, he does not reject the possibility of a German-Jewish relation. But in keeping with his solution to the problem of tolerance quoted earlier, this relation is possible only by recognizing the incommensurability between each side of the hyphen. Rosenzweig criticizes both Mendelssohn and Lessing for taking from Judaism its particularity and its particular language. In doing so, he contends, Judaism became a matter of the past as opposed to living word in the present.

The theme that connects the cultural writings of Franz Rosenzweig collected in this volume is the issue of orientation in the modern world. This issue bridges Rosenzweig's views on pagans, Christians, and Jews, and his views of Moses Mendelssohn, the cultural significance of Lessing, the writing of Stefan George, and even the modern phenomenon of the concert hall on the phonograph record. Moreover, the issue of orientation in the modern world allows us also to connect these cultural writings with some of the major philosophical themes of *The Star of Redemption*. Too often the *Star* has been read as if it were about the possibility of personal revelation. Although revelation can orient the modern person, the essays collected here allow us to appreciate that for Rosenzweig, individual people are also always embodied members of living traditions.

Once again, reference to Gadamer's definition of hermeneutics is helpful: "The nature of the hermeneutical experience is not that something is outside that desires admission. Rather, we are possessed by something and precisely by means of it we are opened up for the new, the different, the true."[12] Rosenzweig argues in the *Star* and beyond that the modern person may well believe that she is discovering revelation anew for herself. Equally important, and too little acknowledged, however, Rosenzweig maintains that the modern person has the possibility of personal encounter only because the historical communities of Jewish and Christian revelation *already* exist in the world, even if she does not know them. Modern people, without knowing it, are for Rosenzweig *already,* to use Gadamer's words, "possessed by something." The hermeneutical arguments of the *Star* and beyond do not suggest that personal revelation makes community possible; rather, they suggest that the historical realities of the Jewish and Christian communities make the experience of revelation possible for the modern person. It is precisely by means of this already having been possessed that we are for Rosenzweig "opened up for the new, the different, the true."[13]

Barbara Galli has again given English readers a great gift by translating Franz Rosenzweig's work into English. Galli first brought English readers Rosenzweig's translations of and commentaries on Judah Halevi's poems' then his lecture notes and essays on God, Man, and World; and then, with Alan Udoff, Rosenzweig's exceptionally important essay "The New Thinking." Now she brings us an important selection of Rosenzweig's cultural writings. English readers will be and should be deeply grateful to Barbara Galli for these unprecedented opportunities to encounter the broad themes and concerns of Rosenzweig's work.

Acknowledgments

Rafael Rosenzweig, for kindly granting permission to publish these works in English.

The evening at the Victor Café, the Music Lovers' Rendezvous on Dickenson Street in Philadelphia

Syracuse University Press, for the spirit of the Director and the marvelous people who work with him

The Leo Baeck Institute, for Dr. Diane Spielmann's warm welcomes

Steven Cahn, for the musical touches

Father, for the belief

Mitch Fenton, for the dignity

Arlene Yusim, for the loyalty

Dennis and Louise Galli, for the opening air

Ken Plax, for his careful, committed, and insightful copyediting

PART ONE

Commentary

1

Introduction

Translating Is a Mode of Holiness

BARBARA E. GALLI

The overarching question in this volume is: What is our appropriate direction, or orientation, in the modern world? The question recurs as a theme and thread throughout Franz Rosenzweig's writings in a cultural vein, translated here for the first time into English. Rosenzweig sees translation as a divine imperative. The third and last part of this introductory essay will consider this directive from the points of view of Rosenzweig (1886–1929), Walter Benjamin (1892–1990), and Franz Kafka.

The second part will highlight the threads of the theme of orientation in the modern world that run through Rosenzweig's cultural writings.

I want to begin, however, by mentioning three thinkers

Written to honor Franz Kafka (1883–1924), who at the time of writing had died seventy years before, on 3 June 1924.

whose works, in my view, cohere with Rosenzweig's. They are Alain Finkielkraut, Gillian Rose (1947–95), and George Steiner (b. 1929, the year Rosenzweig died). The proximity of Finkielkraut to Rosenzweig is evident in *The Defeat of the Mind;* of Gillian Rose in *Mourning Becomes the Law;* and of Steiner most predominantly in *Real Presences.*[1] I am going to concentrate on Steiner, who, unwittingly, has carried on Rosenzweig's work in the cultural sphere, and, who, I would argue (but not here), is the closest in thought and sensibilities to Rosenzweig's among our contemporary intellectuals, closer than Levinas. Moreover, in this specific context, Steiner more than other two is writing with much attention to music; to the prevalence of secondary, commentary speech over primary, creative speaking; to God as a reality; and all this is greatly akin to Rosenzweig.

Steiner and Rosenzweig

Steiner seeks to portray, in *Real Presences,* as does Rosenzweig in *Star of Redemption,* the openly admitted unprovable reality of transcendence and metaphysics. Both argue from the standpoints of common sense and human experience, and language and translation. Nihilistic philosophies, deconstruction, postmodernism all argue for the real as only that which is precisely verifiable. So, sliding deeper into the silent abysses at the edges of all that is unverifiable—for example, language as an organic order; God; meaning; possibilities for interpretation—the end of this century is characterized as lost, as irretrievably impossible to interpret. If interpretation is possible, it is never without grave error.

There is no way out, there is an impasse behind us, ahead of us, above us. Only below is there a way out, only abysses avail meaning that is meaningless. *Real Presences* states a reverse argument. Steiner's book

> proposes that any coherent understanding of what language is and how language performs, that any coherent account of the capacity of human speech to communicate meaning and feeling is, in the final analysis, underwritten by the assumption of God's presence. I will put forward the argument that the experience of aesthetic meaning in particular, that of literature, of the arts, of musical form, infers the necessary possibility of this 'real presence'. The seeming paradox of a 'necessary possibility' is, very precisely, that which the poem, the painting, the musical composition are at liberty to explore and to enact.
>
> This study will contend that the wager on the meaning of meaning, on the potential of insight and response when one human voice addresses another, when we come face to face with the text and work of art or music, which is to say when we encounter the *other* in its condition of freedom, is a wager on transcendence.
>
> This wager—it is that of Descartes, of Kant and of every poet, artist, composer of whom we have explicit record— predicates the presence of a realness, of a 'substantiation' (the theological reach of this word is obvious) within language and form. It supposes a passage, beyond the fictive or the purely pragmatic, from meaning to meaningfulness. The conjecture is that 'God' *is,* not because our grammar is outworn; but that grammar lives and generates worlds because there is the wager on God.[2]

So, like Rosenzweig's, Steiner's is a rare voice in the intellectual world which perceives language as interactive with God, as actually indicative of God as a reality, as a presence.

To Steiner, the breakdown between the correspondence of word and world, the rejection of the poetic challenge to the "sayability" of the world occurred as a unique historical period, "in European, Central European and Russian culture and speculative consciousness during the decades from the 1870s to the 1930s. *It is this break of the covenant between word and world which constitutes one of the very few genuine revolutions of spirit in Western history and which defines modernity itself.*"[3] Many thinkers of the period addressed this: Karl Kraus, Mauthner, Wittgenstein, Hofmannsthal, Schoenberg. Karl Kraus had the sharpest ear: "His ear was so sharp that he caught in the bombast and *kitsch,* in the false lyricism and pseudo-scientific jargon, notably in medicine, of Viennese and Berlin-German prior to and between both World wars, the ground-bass of the nearing disaster. In Karl Kraus, *Sprachkritik* [language criticism] became utter clairvoyance. Listening to the Babel of the *bourse* [stock exchange], to the lies of pundits and politicians, Kraus said, even before 1914, that a time was fast nearing when, in the heartlands of high Western culture and literacy, men would make gloves of human skin."[4] None of those seriously thinking about language at the time regarded language as abstract, as partaking in language-games, as an intellectual curiosity, as a replaceable tool. Each serious thinker on language knew that respecting what we say, and how we hear and receive what others say, is truly a matter of life and death. To Steiner, words go beyond death: word obeys a "principle of the conservation of energy as universal as is that in physics," and that is why: "The irreversibility of the word, once it has been said, haunts many cultures and sensibilities."[5]

To Steiner, as to Rosenzweig, poets and music are the medium to the unprovable metaphysical. Steiner's notions of transcendence, too, are consonant with Rosenzweig's. To Rosenzweig, three irreducible, mutually and equally transcendent elements comprise reality: God, man, world. None collapses into any other. Relation among them is, therefore, requisite, through time, in order to arrive at truths. Meetings are needed. I shall return to this later. Steiner speaks of the need for two freedoms in primary discourse, encounter or meeting, to arrive at a full freedom: freedom of speaker, artist, writer, artwork facing the freedom of respondent, viewer, reader, interpreter.

Most interesting in Steiner's work with regard to translation, for our specific interests here, is his inquiry into the problem of the ethics of the reception of the work of art. "A master translator," says Steiner, "can be defined as a perfect host."[6] Steiner notes that all religion holds in highest regard the acts of welcome and hospitality. He writes of lexical courtesy, *cortesia,* as the first of three steps in translating, in philology: "that which makes us dwellers in the great dictionaries."[7] In this context Steiner refers to Walter Benjamin: "It takes a distinct musicality of interpretative hearing, an ear for temporal tuning such as we find in Coleridge, in Walter Benjamin, in William Empson, to hear, to register with near-perfect or perfect pitch the life of time and of structure within words. . . . Gradually the finesse of our reception increases."[8] The second stage is the sensitivity to syntax and grammars; and, if "one is to give true welcome, into one's own small granary of feeling and of understanding . . . one must be able to hear grammar made music."[9] The third stage is that of the semantic, which "denotes the executive of passage of means into meaning."[10] And yet: "However deep the trust and the disclosure, there are things about our visitant that we shall never know."[11] Given these stages, once welcomed, once translated, the welcomer, the translator, has changed. Something else, literally, has entered him. Translation does transform the world. To Rosenzweig, as we shall see, all speech is translation. Steiner notes that our cities *are* different after Balzac and Dickens; southern European summer nights have changed with Van Gogh.

The parallels and kinships run throughout the thought of Rosenzweig and Steiner, and I feel that I could quote all of *Real Presences.* It is time to turn to Rosenzweig's writings.

Orientation in Rosenzweig's Writings in a Cultural Vein

Orientation in the modern world, to Rosenzweig, involves the direction that starts with and moves from the particular and leads to and ends in the universal. The end, the universal, means peace. Particulars are singularities that cannot be subsumed by other particulars who or that might claim universality, totality. No human being, for instance, is to be swallowed up by any other particular, including God. Nor is God to be swallowed up by any human being. To Rosenzweig, God, human being, and world are the distinct, separate, irreducible elements (freedoms, Steiner would say) of reality. Each is equally transcendent to the other. Just as God is transcendent to us, so too are we transcendent to God. Meeting, then, becomes the way in which to understand, to receive, one another, to bridge without violating

borders, in order to arrive at truths. Time, therefore, nourishes truths. Timeless truths and static truths of logic are
abandoned as unreal, or at most as only an insufficient base
upon which nothing can *happen,* for there is no speaking in
timelessness. Instead, the messiness of meetings; the risk of
not knowing ahead of time what we are going to say because the other person may give us our cue; the unease of
hearing someone else speak *after* we have had our say; the
welcoming of full word as word and response—all this is
embraced in Rosenzweig's proposed orientation in the
modern world.

Moving from the particular voice to the universal chorus
of accord means moving from a beginning to an end. The
cycles of nature, of the seasons, are not infinite (though certain times within may become eternal). The categories of
time (and of not only time) are creation, revelation, and
redemption. On one level, the categories are chronologi-
cally linear. On the other levels, they are temporally en-
twined, each implying, needing the other, in order to make
full sense. In short, the elements of reality—God, human
being, world—relate through time in the categories of creation, revelation, and redemption, and arrive at truths, ultimately Truth, and peace. *The Star of Redemption* is devoted
largely to the explanation of this as the new direction philosophy is to take. With Hegel, according to Rosenzweig,
the two-thousand-year inquiry of Western philosophic tradition has been successfully completed. That is, having an-
swered the questions concerning essence—what is God,
what is the world, what is the human being—philosophy
has completed its task.

New philosophy will be meaningful only if new vital philosophical questions are asked. The new questions are questions of action, time, event: What *happens* between the elements? This narrative method of doing philosophy was the mandate of Schelling. Rosenzweig, in *The Star of Redemption,* proposes to take on the task.

The movements toward peace possible in the new philosophy are manifold. Living according to liturgical calendars is one, as the concluding part of the *Star* details. Dialogue as a moral equivalent to war is another, whether between nations or between individuals. Education as dialogical as well as centered on primary, classical texts, is a third, as Rosenzweig spells out in several writings.[12] Translation, as Rosenzweig means it, is included as a part of all these moves; and on its own translation provides a major path itself. The writings in a cultural vein each reflect in different ways the orientation within translation toward peace.

The colorfully impassioned piece, "Hic et Ubique!" or, "Here and Everywhere!" could well be read in conjunction with *Lost Illusions,* a novel by Balzac (1799–1850).[13] Both Balzac and Rosenzweig, in these texts, see the early capitalistic corruptions of journalism and bookselling. Language, books, and writers are relegated to being debased as only commodities. Capitalism's call for reorientation in the modern world, as Rosenzweig writes in "Hic et Ubique!" is the same whether in peacetime or wartime: "industry and commerce." Rosenzweig illustrates the stagnation of language with a reference to Hamlet's words to Horatio: "The baking from the funeral meal of peace made cold dishes for the marriage feast of the dead."

In "Fighters" Rosenzweig promotes education as *not* learning how to copy thinking, but how to think for oneself. He praises the first series just coming out in 1923, of a "philosophical paperback library," comprising five volumes, containing works by Voltaire, Feuerbach (whom Rosenzweig had named, incidentally, as the discoverer of the new philosophy), Kierkegaard, Schrempf, Dostoyevsky. "Fighters" favorably reviews these works.

With regard to the next very short three writings, on Lessing's *Nathan,* on Lessing's style, and on Mendelssohn, let me just point out that Rosenzweig here asks how empty is this presupposition of the one humanity, as long as human beings are not willing? He looks at a key question in *Nathan:* Are Christian and Jew sooner Christian and Jew than human being? Of the relationship between Moses Mendelssohn, who was baptized as a Christian and whose next generations were likewise baptized, and Lessing, Rosenzweig comments that their friendship was too messianic, and lacked in the blood of the present time. Also here we find Rosenzweig marking differences between tolerance in the Middle Ages and tolerance in the 1920s.

In "Stefan George" Rosenzweig states his belief in the inseparability of intellect (*Geist*) and speech, much in the way Steiner elucidates in *Real Presences* his belief in the organic connection between word and world.

"The Concert Hall on the Phonograph Record" is composed of music reviews of the then new recording technology. They were written during Rosenzweig's last two years, and they are upbeat with a positive light on the possibilities of the vastly increased expansion and accessibility of musical works in private homes, to many more people than ever before. Steiner holds music to be inseparable from the metaphysical and religious feeling, and, as well, to be central to man's access to or abstentions from metaphysical experience; he also holds that to ask what is music is to ask what is man.[14] In my essay following this one, I look at aspects of these reviews, and explicitly relate them to Rosenzweig's philosophy. For the final part of that next essay I focus on Rosenzweig's question raised in connection with all art, and specifically with Mahler's *Kindertotenlieder* (Songs on the death of children): How much are we permitted to let suffering become beauty for us? This question carries in it the questions of translatability of suffering, of the response to another's suffering, and of our attempts at expressing our suffering to others.

Today, of course, among the avenues of orientation in the modern world that are related to speech and translation are those of the various forms of psychotherapy.

Now we turn to the main section of this essay, on translation.

Rosenzweig, Benjamin, Kafka, and the Translation Imperative

By engaging Kafka and Walter Benjamin for this closer focus, I am implicitly demonstrating the concern among German Jews at the time Rosenzweig was writing regarding language and translation, as well as arguing for the cultural relevance of the view that translation can serve as orientation. Further, if Rosenzweig's philosophy of translation is relevant culturally, then the translated writings that follow in this volume can be more easily read as organically connected to both cultural and philosophic-theological concerns.

Seventy years ago, two profound, elusively difficult, Continental thinkers placed translating on the highest philosophical and theological planes. Writing in the second decade and the twenties of this century, between the two World Wars, Rosenzweig and Benjamin predicted and prescribed that the philosophy of the future would be a philosophy of language, with special reference to translation.

In 1923 and 1924, two books comprised of poetry translated into German appeared: Walter Benjamin's translations of Baudelaire's *Tableaux parisiens,* and Franz Rosenzweig's translations of sixty hymns and poems by Jehuda Halevi. Each book contains an essay on the philosophy of translation. About twenty pages each, these two essays, both gems, Benjamin's "The Task of the Translator," written to introduce his Baudelaire book, and Rosenzweig's afterword to his Halevi translations, display similar theories of translation. The principles described are best read in the essays themselves, but I offer them synopsized here.

I will begin with an explanation of an undercurrent, showing up from time to time, quite literally foundationally embedded, piecemeal, in the following footnotes. Quotations from Kafka's *Great Wall of China,* written at the conclusion of the Great War in 1918 or 1919, more effectively than a synopsis or spinning out of the essays could achieve, both clarify and exemplify Rosenzweig's and Benjamin's principles. *The Great Wall of China* was published post-humously, in 1931, and therefore Rosenzweig, already two years dead, did not read it, whereas Benjamin did.

Kafka, Rosenzweig, and Benjamin were all questioning, with urgency, the directions language had taken. Kafka provided his co-seers Rosenzweig and Benjamin, through his uncomfortable writings, the comfort of a kinship. The relatedness among the three precludes and precedes personal meetings; and instead it is as if they were either sharers in or recognizers of the same divine sparks. A metaphysical realm for these three, however distanced or distant, entailed serious responsibility.

Rosenzweig refers only rarely to Kafka, and mostly in letters to his parents, for the first time in 1917. On 25 May 1927, however, he remarked tellingly to his cousin, Gertrud Oppenheim: "The people who wrote the Bible seem to have thought of God much the way Kafka did. I have never read a book that reminded me so much of the Bible as his novel *The Castle,* and that is why reading it certainly cannot be called a pleasure."[15] Given Rosenzweig's collaborative translation of the Bible with Buber, this observation carries much import. In *The Castle* we have the tragic situation of the human being (K), the world (village), and God (castle) when they all exist, but they do not relate, however hard the estranged K might try.

Benjamin's meditations on Kafka, according to Gershom Scholem, held a central position in Benjamin's thought, along with philosophy of language.[16] Scholem does not state the connection, but Benjamin's, as well as Rosenzweig's reflections on Kafka are linked to their theories of translation.

Nahum N. Glatzer observes: "Modern man's condition (presented with ultimate precision by Franz Kafka) is to stand in a world grown silent, waiting for a message that never reaches him—and it is also Rosenzweig's intellectual position."[17] Most of Kafka's stories and novels have to do with messages that move along long paths toward the intended recipient(s) from a hidden position, or person, and that originate from some ultimate, obscure, distant authority, whether divine, legal, bureaucratic, or regal. The theme of the message as harbinger of hope or hopelessness appears in diverse ways from stories and novels as divergent in tone and mood as "The Burrow," "Josephine, the Singing Mouse," "In the Penal Colony," *The Trial,* and *Amerika.*

In *The Great Wall of China* the entire reported action (history) takes place in obedience to an authoritative message called the "high command." The action is secondary to the attempt to understand the command. It is the command that is explicitly analyzed throughout, crafted into Kafka's art by way of a humorously, pretended scholarly method. The principle at the base of the the high command is that of "piecemeal construction" of the wall. This reflects, in architectural language, one of the common areas in the translation theories of both Rosenzweig and Benjamin, and thus *The Great Wall of China* provides a parallel reading. Rosenzweig, Benjamin, and Kafka, as philosopher, cultural critic, and litterateur respectively, say many similar things. Kafka's portrayal of the high command to build the wall runs alongside Rosenzweig's notion of the biblical commandment to strive for and intend toward that one, pure, divine, or true language. Rosenzweig's notion of the one language is directly derived from the command "Love your neighbor." The fulfillment of both the high command and the biblical commandment is not seen as achievable in grand sweeps of timeless logic. Nor can the goal be reached in a grand progressively unifying but deafening crescendo culminating in a final, single, dominant one language. Rather, like the Great Wall that is commanded to be constructed in piecemeal fashion, the one language of truth is being perfected piece by piece, in fragments, in individual languages. Just as with the Wall, only all the interdependent, perfected pieces together can constitute, or institute really, the oneness, and the commanded wholeness of the world, among human beings. At present moments in time, it is not expected that all the pieces physically meet or linguistically join together. For now, the wall-pieces, or the individual languages, each in themselves comprises a whole, or an entirety in germ cell whenever obeying the command to bridge or connect from one to the other. The movement from particular to universal is operative here. If these ways of thinking are ultimately systems, they are not yet complete, and only Rosenzweig among the three, has full faith in the completion; the other two have faith in the need to try.

In this chapter I will place quotations from *The Great Wall of China* in footnotes, separated from the endnotes, as parallels in artistic form or architectural analogy through literature, ways of thinking similar to Benjamin's and Rosenzweig's theories of translation. The first quotation from Kafka, however, will occur in the text, as I want to comment on it. There is the suggestion in the tale of *The Great Wall of China* that the "high command" is issued and is picked up from the point where the building of the Tower of Babel failed. The fulfillment of the "high command" marks the prelude to reaching heaven. This time the imperative reaches out to a multiplicity of languages and nations, with the divine intention to unify them, and to protect them. In the story *The Great Wall of China,* it is recounted that a scholar had long ago researched, not merely written documents, but also the site of the Tower, and had concluded that "the Great Wall alone would provide for the first time in the history of mankind a secure foundation for a new Tower of Babel. First the wall, therefore, and then the tower. . . . How could the wall, which did not form even a circle, but only a sort of quarter or half-circle, provide the foundation for a tower?" the tale-teller asks, and decides: "That could obviously be meant only in a spiritual sense."[18] True, the tale-teller then calls it one wild idea among many, but in the tone of when one immediately after a statement of a genuine feeling or opinion, attempts to take it back. The listener believes the statement and not the subsequent attempt to brush it aside as irrelevant.

As building the wall in piecemeal fashion was to eventuate in a wholeness, so translating, to Rosenzweig and Benjamin, was to lead to the wholeness of pure language. They each deepened these convictions through the course of their own translating activities.

Rosenzweig

On 23 December 1922, upon completion of translating "two magnificent poems" by Halevi, Rosenzweig wrote in a letter to Martin Buber (1878–1965): "[T]here's no getting away from it: one's time is better spent in translating ten lines than writing the longest disquisition about."[19] The Halevi book was published in the spring of 1924, and on 1 April of that year, also to Buber, Rosenzweig commented: "I have always said: for my translations I'll go to heaven, I expect no reward on earth."[20] To his close friend Margarete Susman, who understood his work intimately, Rosenzweig wrote on 22 August 1924: "I myself understand a poem only after I have translated it; a compromising confession."[21] He meant all these statements seriously. Speech is at the heart of his philosophy. To him, all speech is translation.[22] Only through the efforts and the effects of translation do we partake in, move toward, but still *within* the multiplicity of languages and peoples, the one language of humankind. In the afterword to the translations, Rosenzweig writes: "That such a renewal of a language through a foreign one is at all possible certainly presupposes that just as the language itself has given birth to each of its speakers, so too all human speaking [*Sprechen*], all foreign language which ever were spoken and ever will be spoken, are contained in it in germ-cell at least. And that is the case. There is only one language. There is no language trait of one language that does not evidence itself, at least in germ, in every other language, be it in dialects, nurseries, peculiarities of trades."[23] Each language *individually* has the capacity to grow into that one language. Each language, in seed, is already that one language. Rosenzweig's notion of there being only one language is an objective philosophical conclusion, a theological statement based on the first chapter of Genesis, and a statement of faith. In Rosenzweig's philosophy, all these "ands" are permitted, even encouraged.

Rosenzweig had several names for his post-Hegelian philosophy: he called it the "and" philosophy; the new thinking (*das neue Denken*); speech-thinking (*Sprachdenken*); experiential philosophy (*erfahrende Philosophie*); and grammatical thinking. If he must choose an "ism" as a label, he says "the designation I would soonest accept would be that of absolute empiricism."[24] Rosenzweig (along with Benjamin) has been called a mystic by scholars from diverse fields such as Robert Alter, Douglas Robinson, Eliezer Schweid,[25] and, as a mystic, is simultaneously characterized also as an unteachable, incomprehensible thinker. Clearly, however, this is not Rosenzweig's own self-conception; not only was it *not* his desire to be obscure, but he especially regarded himself as a practical thinker whose thought was tied to life experience. His aims to be understood can be abundantly documented.[26] He was therefore repeatedly dismayed and disappointed whenever he was not understood, especially with respect to his Halevi book. He believed he had served this book to his readers in tempting hors d'oeuvres fashion by the accompaniment of the notes. He states in the afterword that the notes were meant mainly to entice the reader to linger over each poem, so that each was enjoyed as one enjoys a peach, not as cherries, quickly, one after the other. Moreover, in the same vein as Steiner, in connection with his study of the ethics of reception, Rosenzweig too sees translating as within the sphere of welcome and hospitality. In his afterword to his translations of the Halevi poetry, Rosenzweig explains the main purpose of the reflective, philosophical notes he writes for each poem: "to induce the reader to take each poem as a thing for itself, just as the poet has composed it as a thing for itself and just as the singer and the hearer, in the place for which it is meant, sang and heard it, sings and hears it, will sing and hear it. Thus, to change the reader from a reader and consumer into a guest and friend of the poem."[27] Concerning the afterword, on 17 June 1924, Rosenzweig complains to Buber: "The strange thing, which I knew from the beginning, is that only the epilogue [afterword] prevents the reader from rejecting the book out of hand. Now practically everyone feels guilty for not having liked the poems. Everybody reads it for the sake of its cheek."[28]

Rosenzweig's presentation and explication of his language-based philosophical system are set out in the three parts of *The Star of Redemption*. Everything happens, as briefly mentioned already, under the theological categories of creation, revelation, and redemption. I shall reiterate this here. The term "happens" is important to Rosenzweig. His primary philosophical question is not "What is the essence of a thing?" but instead "What happens? What story is being told? What world story is unfolding?" Concluding in part I of the *Star* that there are three irreducible elements of reality, and that each of them is equally transcendent to the other—God, man and world—Rosenzweig brings this cast onto the stage of part II where the action begins. We come to know and arrive at truths, and ultimately Truth, through linguistic relationship, and in time as characterized by the categories of creation, revelation, and redemption. Examples of the practical application of this theoretical philosophic system are Rosenzweig's two major works on translation: his Bible translation in collaboration with Martin Buber,[29] and his translations of poems by Jehuda Halevi.

Walter Benjamin

Walter Benjamin, too, envisioned the coming philosophy as one to be steered by a theory of language, although with him, we have no systematically developed philosophy; no voluminous collection of letters. We do have his copious writings, mainly in the form of essays and articles in the pioneering areas of literary, social, and cultural criticism. These seldom deal directly, overtly, with language. But behind and beneath the writings stands his philosophy of language: the introduction to the Baudelaire book, "The Task of the Translator," was for Benjamin his credo. All these other writings, even those written before "The Task of the Translator," speak with the principles and tenets expressed in that introductory essay.

For Benjamin communicability is the content of language: language communicates communicability.[30] Translatability is the essential feature of certain works. For example, literary artworks impart truths; truths do not merely merit, but are destined to have continued life.[31] That which is absolutely translatable, therefore, is Truth in unfragmented form, as in holy writings. Essentially, then, translatable works are related to the divine essence, or what is imparted of it in divine revelation. The linguistic categories of communicability and translatability, however, are again, as for Rosenzweig, objective, and not mystical categories.[32] Translation is a mode (*Form*) that intends toward "pure language." A literary work of art, insofar as it contains truth, then, in linguistic form, would be communicable, and, insofar as it is expressive of a truth or truths, would be translatable. If the intention in translation is toward "pure language," then the intention is toward neither the original nor toward the translating language, but rather toward something that is *in* each language concerned, and as well *beyond* each. The metaphysical realm is present in language. "Because of its direction [*Richtung*], a translation is not called upon by the original work of art for the sake of that work itself, but rather for the benefit of pure, or divine language itself."[33]

"Pure language" is a term first used in German in the philosophical context of linguistic theory by Friedrich von Humboldt (1767–1835),[34] and by his contemporary, Friedrich Hölderlin (1770–1843), the most gifted of translators and sublimest of poets. Benjamin interchanges the term "pure language" with the terms "one true language," "divine language," and "a language of truth." The supreme philosophic endeavor, he says, strives for this expression of truth *in* language:

> If there is such a thing as a language of truth, the tensionless and even silent depository of the ultimate truth which all thought strives for, then this language of truth is the true language. And this very language, whose divination and description is the only perfection a philosopher can hope for, is concealed in concentrated fashion in translations. There is no muse of philosophy, nor is there one of translation. But despite the claims of sentimental artists, these two are not banausic [i.e., lowbrow, philistine]. For there is a philosophic genius that is characterized by a yearning for that language which manifests itself in translations.[35]

Similarities Between Rosenzweig and Benjamin

There are differences between Rosenzweig and Benjamin in their theories of language and of translation. Benjamin sees a deterioration in spoken language from an originally pure Logos, whereas Rosenzweig sees no such degeneration.* Benjamin does, however, call Holy Scripture absolutely translatable Truth, and thus, though he does not state it, he does see one—unspoken—language, as already perfected. Humboldt favours one, that is, Sanskrit, and Rosenzweig does make the claim that one language is already perfect: Biblical Hebrew. The differences and parallels between Benjamin and Rosenzweig have been carefully charted in a characteristically clear, comparative essay by the thorough scholarship of the renowned Rosenzweig interpreter, Stéphane Mosès.[36] I have no intention of here ignoring, minimizing, or sweeping aside the importance of the differences defined by Mosès.

The reason I want to consider here the similarities alone is that in this way I might better uncover the senses of holiness, apartness or metaphysicality, in the language theories.

---

* "The farther one descends among the lower schools the more, naturally enough, does one find teachers' and pupils' doubts of their own knowledge vanishing, and a superficial culture mounting sky high round a few precepts that have been drilled into people's minds for centuries, precepts which, though they have lost nothing of their eternal truth, remain eternally invisible in this fog of confusion" (*The Great Wall*, p. 82).

The places where Benjamin and Rosenzweig do meet are those holy places where the holiness in translating is sensed. With the lightest and most transparent of touches, translating covers the grounds of both holy place and holy time. Time does not, by nature, stand still, nor, by its nature, does a translation of a work of art, of a fragment of Truth. A translation represents a life stage in the hallowed growth of a truth (Truth) in a language.*

To recognize a holy place, or a holy time, creates a remarkable effect. Rosenzweig's afterword and Benjamin's "Task of the Translator" were effectively created out of the recognition of spatial and temporal sacredness in translating. Pausing in the pages of these two essays leaves one different, changed, from beforehand, even if one had had beforehand a consciousness of language's creativeness and expressiveness. It is not any mystic element or tone or content or influence that affects the reader of these essays, but the controlled fervor, the certainty with which these indisputably superior, wholesome, and respectable intellects carry and urge their points. Pausing with Benjamin and Rosenzweig on the lapping shores of language where language borders shimmeringly break, for a bright moment, during the transit of translating, makes a lasting difference in one's life, in one's daily speaking and hearing of language.[37] Finding the similarities certainly does not obliterate the differences once perceived, but does eventuate a change in the difference:

---

*"Battles that are old history are new to us, and one's neighbour rushes in with a jubilant face to tell the news" (*The Great Wall*, p. 85).

they appear now to be differences of direction and not of path.*

Because the goal—end—fulfillment, according to each thinker, for each language, is always both above and below the path, and because these other planes constitute the end, then the image for language growth must be pictured in the following way: the multiplicity of languages remains intact; no one language is subsumed by any other. For the translating language that has opened for a new spirit, as crucial as its opening has been, equally crucial is its reclosing, for the moment, of its own language borders. Each language grows upward like a tree—only if it strengthens and deepens its own roots can it grow upward. Its roots *must* grow deeper in order to rise to the area of aboveness. The "end," "goal," "fulfillment" is *not* that of all languages *meeting*, but rather that of each reaching the same depth and height—of Truth,

---

*"The Great Wall of China was finished off at its northernmost corner. From the south-east and the south-west it came up in two sections that finally converged there. This principle of piecemeal construction was also applied on a smaller scale by both of the two great armies of labour, the eastern and the western. It was done in this way: gangs of some twenty workers were formed who had to accomplish a length, say of five hundred yards of wall, while a similar gang built another stretch of the same length to meet the first. But after the junction had been made the construction of the wall was not carried on from the point, let us say, where this thousand yards ended; instead the two groups of workers were transferred to begin building again in quite different neighbourhoods" (*The Great Wall,* p. 72).

one by one, in its own time and its own place. The achievement of smaller goals, and the life stages of truths that are manifested in each new translation, may be celebrated.*

Four areas of convergence occur explicitly in Benjamin's and Rosenzweig's writings on language. First, they both reject any claim that language is an instrument. Second, they perceive a *life* in the growth of language, which, through translation, leads toward the pure or one language. Third, they connect language growth directly with peace and redemption. Fourth, they maintain that Holy Scriptures are imperatively and unconditionally translatable, *and* are at the same time the security against getting lost in language, against untruthful translation.

They developed and learned their respective theories of language out of their own experiences in translating works of art, poems. This area of convergence, then, is primarily experiential, and secondarily rational thought or later reflection; but Rosenzweig and Benjamin, on both primary and

---

*"[T]he hopelessness of such hard toil which yet could not reach completion even in the longest lifetime, would have cast them into despair and above all made them less capable for the work. It was for this reason that the system of piecemeal building was decided on. . . . Accordingly, while they were still exalted by the jubilant celebrations marking the completion of the thousand yards of wall, they were sent far, far away, saw on their journey finished sections of the wall rising here and there, came past the quarters of the high command and were presented with badges of honour. . . . All this assuaged their impatience" (*The Great Wall*, p. 75).

secondary counts, meet on similar holy ground. Theory here follows practice, or emerges from it organically.* The universal is arrived at from the particular, which for them is the accurate reflection of reality. So it happens in the Creation story, the particulars precede the universal.[38]

As well as from the experience of translating, their keenly urgent concern for and intensive interest in language also arose from their knowledge that language's holy ground was in severe danger of being desecrated further than it already had been by events leading up to, through and beyond 1914–18. In turn, in the closing decade of this century we face escalated concerns: on the one hand, repressive regimes rage virulently, much controlled by propagandistic and censored journalism; on the other hand, valiant fights for freedom in parts of the globe very distant from one another demonstrate the unifying power of speech, and the powers of truth that through new speech catch hold in the earth and blaze ever higher.

I shall now proceed as follows. (1) I shall look at some difficulties regarding Rosenzweig's and Benjamin's essays, in respect of their time of publication, and of today. (2) I shall

---

*"Far rather do I believe that the high command has existed from all eternity, and the decision to build the wall likewise. Unwitting peoples of the north, who imagined they were the cause of it! Honest, unwitting Emperor, who imagined he decreed it! We builders of the wall know that it was not so and hold our tongues." *The Great Wall*, p. 81.

try to give a sense of the types of concerns and proposed correctives about language of other thinkers of the period, especially in connection with the shocks and aftershocks of World War I, through brief quotations. (3) I shall consider more closely the four areas of convergence listed above, that is: (a) rejection of instrumentalist views of language, (b) notions of language growth, (c) links between language growth and peace, and (d) Scripture as safeguard of truth in translating. (4) I shall conclude with a consideration of the essays as possibly vital resources for today's thinkers, especially with regard to what seems now to be a dualized world that fights for a robustly welcoming pluralism, and one that mocks daily and in new evilly ingenious ways the notion—fact—divine command—of pluralism, of languages, faiths, peoples.*

The Essays and the Difficulties

Benjamin was pleased with and proud of his essay, "The Task of the Translator." On 26 May 1921, that is, two years prior to the Baudelaire book's publication, he wrote to Ger-

---

*"During the building of the wall and ever since to this very day I have occupied myself almost exclusively with the comparative history of races—there are certain questions which one can probe to the marrow, as it were, only by this method—and I have discovered that we Chinese possess certain folk and political institutions that are unique in their clarity, others again unique in their obscurity. The desire to trace the causes of these phenomena, especially the latter, has always teased me and teases me still, and the building of the wall is itself essentially involved with these problems" (*The Great Wall*, p. 81).

shom Scholem: "To my great joy and relief I was recently able to write the preface to the Baudelaire translation." Scholem characterizes the essay, "The Task of the Translator," as a high point, when Benjamin's "approach to the philosophy of language was openly theological in orientation. He attached particular importance to these pages, viewing them as something like his credo; to be sure, the study contained all the ingredients that gained for his writings the reputation of incomprehensibility."[39]

Rosenzweig, like Benjamin, as we shall see, suffered a similar reputation during his lifetime, and expressed the pain of being unheard and unread with equal consternation. In neither case do the reasons for the difficulties have anything to do with an inability to construct grammatically clear sentences, or with an inelegance or sloppiness of style, as has been the case for many a worthy "new" thinker, for instance, Humboldt himself. Both Benjamin and Rosenzweig expressed themselves in exquisite German. Each had new things to say, and therefore had to utter his words in a new, unfamiliar order of speaking. Yet, they both did this with old words, with plain language. With Rosenzweig and Benjamin it is their newness, that is, the unfamiliarity of their thought, that is difficult to follow. Creative with language, certainly, but, unlike the (valuable) work of the deconstructionists, Rosenzweig and Benjamin were not self-consciously creating a new language and in this way meaning to make the reader stumble and think anew. Unlike deconstructionists, they are not desirous of dissecting language to learn more about it; the difference Benjamin and Rosenzweig want to make is the internal expansion of language borders, the growth of truth in each language. True, they do not spin out their thoughts; the trellis of thought-work is tight. Not a sentence, not a word can be spared. One often wishes for longer verbal spaces between the intensely profound terrain, for more flatland, more planes of explanation. As students, scholars, and interpreters of both thinkers know, the depths of Rosenzweig's and Benjamin's philosophic insights and sublimely controlled flights of thought concerning metaphysical or transcendent realms are dismissed with annoyance as mystical or exclusive to initiates; or, at the far other end of reaction, are returned to again and again. This latter reaction is like turning again and again to scriptural passages that allure in their elusiveness in the steady comprehending of the moving depths and heights of the contoured text.

As with great artworks, familiarity with the depths of these thinkers does not make understanding easier. Their thought, even once grasped, remains elusive. Thought that approaches the divine always is elusive, unless it is "proving" God, for the divine can never, we know, be grasped, touched, contained, comprehended, seen. The human approach must be *permitted* or called or commanded by divine willing, or in answer to a human plea. Authentic thought— and genuine speech—must always attempt to approach the divine, to draw as close as possible. The propriety of degrees and kinds of closeness varies from moment to moment. We know we cannot face God and live. The propriety, plan of approach needs to be approved, invited even, by divine imperative beforehand. Being aware of the proximity of sacred ground in another's language that requires—demands approach, can alone prepare the way for approach: to this awareness a divine reaction may occur, may be granted.*

*". . . when we discovered that without the high command

Language can face God and live. It lives only and precisely by this facing. The world's Holy Scriptures do this. Language, humanly spoken, can approach God, and the speaker lives.

In the essays there are places of brushing against the divine, touching shimmering realms open only to language. Benjamin's and Rosenzweig's own cautious footsteps lead the way to approach a place where these touches might be lightly felt, like the fingers of the artist touching the strings of a holy harp, and we who wish to follow can lose our balance, develop dizziness, stumble and fall.

For all the safety in language, too much care can never be taken when in the realms of translating. Benjamin reminds us that the language gates closed on Hölderlin the translator, surrounding him with silence. But, as with Benjamin and Rosenzweig, a divine hand might steady our course.*

---

neither our book learning nor our human understanding would have sufficed for the humble tasks which we performed in the great whole. In the office of the command . . . one may be certain that all human thoughts and desires were revolved, and counter to them all human aims and fulfillments. And through the window the reflected splendours of divine worlds fell on the hands of the leaders as they traced their plans" (*The Great Wall*, p. 78).

*"In those days many people, and among them the best, had a secret maxim which ran: Try with all your might to comprehend the decrees of the high command, but only up to a certain point; then avoid further meditation. A very wise maxim, which moreover was elaborated in a parable that was later often quoted: Avoid further meditation, but not because it might be harmful; it is not

There was no fear of anyone growing dizzy in considering Benjamin's principles in "The Task of the Translator" when it first appeared. "The utter silence with which this essay was received constituted [Benjamin's] first great disappointment on the literary plane," Gershom Scholem tells us. "The sole exception was a ludicrously vacuous statement by Stefan Zweig."[40]

Rosenzweig's theories of language as presented in *The Star of Redemption* incidentally had no influence on Benjamin at the time of his writing of "The Task of the Translator."[41] Benjamin's own entry into Rosenzweig's thought, though Scholem had encouraged Benjamin to read the *Star* as early as 1921, really occurred only after the appearance of the second edition of the *Star,* in 1930, just after Rosen-

---

at all certain that it would be harmful. What is harmful or not harmful has nothing to do with the question. Consider rather the river in spring. It rises until it grows mightier and nourishes more richly the soil on the long stretch of its banks, still maintaining its own course until it reaches the sea, where it is all the more welcome because it is a worthier ally.—Thus far may you urge your meditations on the decrees of the high command.—But after that the river overflows its banks, loses outline and shape, slows down the speed of its current, tries to ignore its destiny by forming little seas in the interior of the land, damages the fields, and yet cannot maintain itself for long in its new expanse, but must run back between its banks again, must even dry up wretchedly in the hot season that presently follows.—Thus far may you not urge your meditations on the decrees of the high command" (*The Great Wall*, pp. 78–79).

zweig's death. Rosenzweig and Benjamin met face to face only once, when Benjamin visited Rosenzweig briefly in Frankfurt. Nothing of import took place. No correspondence developed, and Rosenzweig left no written mention of the visit.

The Shocked Linguistic Atmosphere

Rosenzweig and Benjamin had been trying to penetrate the clouds of mystery around language for at least ten years prior to writing their essays on translation. They were especially asserting mystery with regard to language in the sense of perpetual and ultimate impenetrability. The mystery "in" language rests not merely in a divine aspect inherent in language; for they see language as both human and divine. It is this human-divine sharing that is the mystery. The communicability, the translatability between the human and the divine is that which constitutes the impossible in translating, and is the only reason for the imperative to translate.

As already emphasized, Benjamin and Rosenzweig are representative of a surge, almost an eruption, of passionate inquirers into theories of language during the years surrounding the two World Wars, most notably the second decade, the twenties and the early thirties of this century, centerd around, but not restricted to, writers working in the German language.[42]

German speakers were proud of their language, brimful of translations, from the English Shakespeare, the Italian Dante, to the Russian Dostoevsky, vast, too, in its own richness of poetic genius, a language towering tall in realms of ethereal purity, drawn up to these realms by Schiller, Goethe, Höl-derlin. When such a towering language coarsens, cracks, crumbles—through lying, thus faltering speech, propagan-distic Babel, falsifying censorship, divisive and destructive—and never unites like speech of truth, the crash breaks through that language's own borders and casts trespassing cascades of disordered debris onto others' linguistic territory.

Thus, the linguistic concerns of post–World War II thinkers and litterateurs, especially those writing in German, such as Günter Grass, Martin Walser, Heinrich Böll, for example, differed from those of the pre–World War I thinkers. The litterateurs' concerns needed to take into ac-count the grave trespasses against not only the German lan-guage but against others' languages, both personal and national, as well. Whether the differences were of kind or of degree is not the issue. As litterateurs, they always find their interest in the human story, the nature of the human, against various backgrounds from the historical to the psychologi-cal. That is to say, similar questions were being asked with regard to meaning in and of language. But the post–World War II era did bring sharp, if not absolute difference, the character of which many Jews and non-Jews, philosophers, theologians, historians, survivors, mourners, poets are still attempting to address, if not to understand.

Post–World War I thinkers, the "new thinkers," such as the contributors to journals like *Der Jude* and *Die Kreatur,* were all concerned, too, with broken language, and the event of 1914 to 1918 confirmed that meaning, and there-fore philosophical inquiry, was tied directly and firmly to event. If language is to be questioned in terms of event, then the mode of approach to linguistic theory or to active language use needs to differ from an approach deriving solely from logic, which cannot embrace the categories of event and time.*

The difference brought about by World War II is the difference of an arguably absolutely unprecedented event: the Holocaust. No linguistic reference points seemed to exist in the resources of language for the survivors, for witnesses, for those others of us who have learned and are learning of an event involving six million murders of Jews, in an aim of the total eradication of a people on earth, and involving as well another five million murders, of gypsies, of homosexuals, of Nazi dissenters. Gillian Rose's *Mourning Becomes the Law* finds linguistic resources to philosophize lucidly with regard to mourning the losses this century knows.

Heinrich Böll tried to collect from the ashen debris protesting ways to create short, incontestably clear sentences. Twistings, tortuous tortures, lingering lies could not be borne forward, if there were to be future speakers.

The mode in Günter Grass becomes that of a bitter, tragic irony, where alienation is no longer a question of the *condition humaine* that is lamented, and lamented as such, as condition, as something fluctuating, perhaps, but definable. As definable, alienation is limited and limiting of the human soul and the human spirit, which are now boxed up in a

---

*"So vast is our land that no fable could do justice to its vastness, the heavens can scarcely span it—and Peking is only a dot in it, and the imperial palace less than a dot" (*The Great Wall,* p. 82).

condition, with no outlet toward hope or possibilities for expansion of boundaries, and thus must turn inward to despair. The well-chosen title of a play, a play in itself, by the alienationist playwright Jean-Paul Sartre tells of the horror of the nature of *condition: Huis-clos, No Exit,* a true hell. In Sartre's writings "action" is actionless, a mimesis of *condition,* of stasis, nonaction.

World War I brought out notions of alienation as a condition. Alienation in World War II was no longer condition but a human mechanism activated to active murder. Condition became event. Now alienation had to be considered, portrayed, spoken of, through the category of event and not only of condition. With alienation as event, the questions concerning alienation develop into ones that face alienation as an active human desire: volitional, systematic acts to alienate that which is different to the point of extinction, annihilation, or extermination. The word *alienation* delivers up not only meanings of passivity: a person has been alienated, a person is in a state of alienation. It is also an active noun. The desire for otherness, to alienate, rests in the word itself, and it betokens the failure of speech, an emptying of its inherently translatable intentions.*

---

*"Now one of the most obscure of our institutions is that of the empire itself. . . . But it is precisely this question of the empire which in my opinion the common people should be asked to answer, since after all they are the empire's final support. . . . True . . . we are always trying to get information on this subject [of the Emperor], but, strange as it may sound, it is almost impossible to discover anything, either from pilgrims, though they have wan-

Thus, for the post–World War II thinkers, the affirmation of language was an agonizing task burdened with a painful process of impossibilities that in their hands was made possible. Their bravery in their work with broken tools can only be deeply respected. That which had been broken, language, could be mended only by language. Language has no replacement. The direct witnesses among the post–World War II thinkers and menders and poets everywhere—Paul Celan, Elie Wiesel, Emil Fackenheim, Steven T. Katz, Gillian Rose, to name too few—all, for whatever hope, explanation, *Tikkun* (Hebrew, to heal), faith-in-spite-of-all, that might be present in their testimonials and works of art—for all this, there remains, and there is emitted, and echoed, in their audiences, a scream that, because silent, cannot yet find an end in the world.

Visually translated, Yad Vashem (the Holocaust memorial in Israel) is that silent scream. But here the distant lights of the stars, the souls, themselves soften the harsh silence from the gently gathering in memory of even those who are not remembered.[43]

Where, other than in divine memory, is hallowed silence permitted or possible? The horrors spilled out into the world during World War II are collected in many worlds, scholarly worlds, art worlds, architectural worlds of memo-

---

dered through many lands, or from near or distant villages, or from sailors, though they have navigated not only our little stream, but also the sacred rivers. One hears a great many things, true, but can gather nothing definite" (*The Great Wall,* pp. 81–82).

rials. Memorials are intended to honor the memory of particular souls; memorials are embodiments of a prayer for peace for these souls. The need for memorials shows also the need for effective, visible, concrete protest against the horrors of the Holocaust being collected as variant reenactments: the proliferation of genocidal manias of the twentieth century. Each mania is its own particular *novum,* perhaps a variant or new deviant growing out of the pieces of debris from the *novum novorum.*[44] Breaking the silence of the silent scream, as Robert Gibbs characterizes the soundless pain out of the Holocaust in his *Correlations in Rosenzweig and Levinas,* are the piercing screams of new victims, new mourners, of deaths and lives made abominable. Resounding screams from increasingly wretchedly complicated places prolong the silence and defy the metaphysical claims and demands that are incumbent on language, on its speakers.

A difference between silent screams and resounding screams blends into an open-eyed helpless mixture of disbelief and of sad knowing.

Events again become condition. Does condition end? Is mourning a condition? Death is an event, mourning is not. If condition, like event, can evoke a meaning of enduring-for-a-while, a needed duration beyond the unstoppable cascade of events, a place for pause between, then a return to eventful life is awaited, welcomed. So Gillian Rose speaks.[45]

Rosenzweig and Benjamin were somewhat Cassandra-like in the situation of the widespread unhearkening hearers surrounding their isolated circles of illumination. Yet they were unlike Cassandra in their innocence; their gift of sight had not been inflicted as a punishment, nor did they have to witness that which they were working, in part, to prevent. Benjamin was self-conscious of his special sight. His *Angelus Novus,* a watercolor by Paul Klee, purchased in 1921 in Munich, was his favorite painting. This New Angel, with its back to the future, its eyes to the past, is hurled toward the future, helplessly witnessing the horrors, destructions, of the present.[46] Is this New Angel a messenger of God? With what message does such an Angel appear to us?* Was the Angelus Novus present for the Holocaust, and is he still present, watching, staring with the eyes of Hölderlin's "blessed immortals," with the eyes of eternal clarity, in absentia, from his ever distancing, ever advancing vantage-point?[47] The Angelus Novus reflects in his eyes the terror (of evil) of the possibility of of event rigidifying into condition.

Neither Rosenzweig nor Benjamin experienced World War II.[48] Those who inquired into language before the second great and terrible World War that raged in Europe—too dreadful anywhere—in important ways can be claimed to be foreseers, through language, of impending further

---

*"If from such appearances any one should draw the conclusion that in reality we have no Emperor, he would not be far from the truth. Over and over again it must be repeated: There is perhaps no people more faithful to the Emperor than ours in the south, but the Emperor derives no advantage from our fidelity. True, the sacred dragon stands on the little column at the end of our village, and ever since the beginning of human memory it has breathed out its fiery breath in the direction of Peking in token of homage—but Peking itself is far stranger to the people in our village than the next world" (*The Great Wall,* p. 87).

dangers in Europe. These were sure to occur unless contemporary philosophical errors were addressed. There is a cry these days against reductionist philosophies, philosophies that reduce everything to one element, philosophies that proceed from the universal to the particular, because, when translated into political and nationalistic terms, these philosophies legitimate totalizing and totalitarian régimes, that reject otherness, or pluralism. Alain Finkielkraut, in *The Defeat of the Mind,* notes, in his view, the overpopularization of antitotalizing attitudes, which has necessarily become facile and lies in its own way. Many people pretend racism is not there (here). Elitism, hierarchies, superiorities, and inferiorities in people and in activities and in the arts are the enemy. In a pretended and preached total acceptance of otherness, ironically, another brand of totalization ensues, he argues.[49]

Neither Rosenzweig nor Benjamin bore, or could bear, in bodily memory that which was not yet embodied in the world and that which was more horrible than anyone could have foreseen: not a oneness of peace, but an endeavor to unite in evil. Their writings bear no memory of that night unbordered by dawns. Their world, even in the darkening light of that night's dusk, holds, for all of us who breathe after that night, a material, physical wholeness and even a wholesomeness. They could maintain, for all their seriousness and foresight into an endangered future, a vision of wholeness in which their energies concentrated. The ultimacy of peace shines through their writings.*

*"[H]ardly ever have I found in my travels such pure morals as

Other thinkers of the period, writing in German, also trusted in language as both a living entity with which human beings could create realities, and a creative life force in itself out of which could be created situations for good or evil.

> On 18–19 February 1913, Kafka wrote to Felice: The wrong sentences lie in wait about my pen, twine themselves around its point, and are dragged along into the letters. I am not of the opinion that one can ever lack the power to express perfectly what one wants to write or say. Observations on the weakness of language, and comparisons between the limitations of words and the infinity of feelings, are quite fallacious. The infinite feeling continues to be as infinite in words as it was in the heart. What is clear within is bound to become so in words as well. This is why one need never worry about language, but at sight of words one may often worry about oneself. After all, who knows within himself how things really are with him? This tempestuous or floundering or morasslike inner self is what we really are, but by the secret process by which words are forced out of us, our self-knowledge is brought to light, and though it may still be veiled, yet it is there before us, wonderful or terrible to behold.[50]

Robert Musil (1880–1942), of Vienna, famed for writing the world's longest novel, *The Man Without Qualities,* echoes that view held by Benjamin, that language has deteriorated from a once pristine state, and that its communicability is

---

in my native village. But yet a life that is subject to no contemporary law, and attends only to the exhortations and warnings which come to us from olden times" (*The Great Wall,* p. 87).

the "residue of the creative word of God."[51] Just as for both Benjamin and Rosenzweig, for Musil, too, language is divine: "There's some great intoxication emanating from the Word, an obscure memory, and sometimes one wonders if everything we experience isn't just scraps of some ancient wholeness of things destroyed long ago, shreds that we once fixed together into one piece again and got it all wrong."[52] Musil's main theme is lack of unity in the modern world: there is no longer a whole man confronting a whole world. Evoking images of frightened, wide-eyed, New Angels with powerless wings, "this atomized world is rushing with brimming energy, like a stellar constellation, toward some terrible unknown goal."[53] Reflected in this atomized world is atomized language.

Another Viennese, Karl Kraus (1874–1936), a brilliant, uncompromising, inspiring thinker, fought bravely with words against war, for the goodness of the human spirit. Karl Kraus's *The Last Days of Mankind: A Tragedy in Five Acts,* is a portrayal of the monstrosity of war, consisting largely of quotations actually written or spoken. In his introduction to the abridged English edition, the editor, Frederick Ungar, writes:

> Kraus' conception of language is of central importance in understanding both the man and his work. He saw the ubiquitous divorce of language and meaning as a major modern dilemma. His relationship to language was of a magic and religious character: the word as magic substitutes for the thing, the linking together of words as a formula possessing magic power. Language for him was not just a means of communication, but rather creative in itself. Kraus

firmly believed that there is a pre-established harmony of word and world, and that the cosmos of one is reflected in the other. . . .

Because he considered language a direct index of morality, Kraus elevated it to man's essential concern, to which every other consideration should be subordinated. In its use of language he saw the cultural strength or weakness of a nation and the carrier of its spirit. Kraus firmly believed that purification of language would work to purify ethics.[54]

On speech and translation, this often cutting writer never wrote disparagingly of language itself, only of abusers, of journalists, Kraus's prime target. Translation was a serious matter to him: "A work of language translated into another language means that a person crosses the border without his skin, and across there puts on the country's national costume [Ein Werk der Sprache in eine andere Sprache übersetzt, heißt, daß einer ohne seine Haut über die Grenze kommt, und drüben, die Tracht des Landes anzieht]."[55] To Kraus, clearly, as to Rosenzweig, "Speech is the mother, not the maid of thought [Die Sprache ist die Mutter, nicht die Magd des Gedankens]."[56]

Convergences

Rejection of Instrumentalist Views of Language. Both Rosenzweig and Benjamin see language as wholly adequate for expression of truth. Language itself is directly the expression of truth, of love. Language is not mere tool, nor mere signifier of something it wants to express beyond itself. Language is capable of expressing anything within itself, spiritual matters as well as material. Language is not that limping, limited, faulty tool incapable of giving expression even of God. In his article on biblical anthropomorphisms, with characteristic passionate humor, Rosenzweig urges his point by asking with which "tool" would we replace language?

> "Inadequacy of language," "limitation of thought," "our sensory experience," finally as a highlight the "God" formed by man in his image—this is how a theological problem is dealt with today! Even if we grant the soundness of these "theoretical-knowledge" imperfections (I frankly do not understand with which language, which thought, which experience we can compare our language, our thought, our experience in order to be permitted to confer upon them the grade of unsatisfactory). Even if we do grant that, in which other science is it permitted to put "theoretical-knowledge" lamentations in the place of honest striving after the understanding of the facts themselves?[57]

From his reading of the Song of Songs as the focal book of revelation, Rosenzweig characterizes revelatory language as more than analogy, more than simile. The essentiality of revelation is recognized in the presentness of experience. Until the advent of the nineteenth century, it was, according to Rosenzweig, unquestioned that "God's word must contain the relationship of lover to beloved directly, the significant, that is, without any pointing to the significate," and that "the distinction between immanence and transcendence disappears in language."[58]

Benjamin's views on the noninstrumentality of language are best told in Hannah Arendt's own poetic way of thinking and with her unique attentiveness to Benjamin. In the following quotation, the references are to "The Task of the Translator":

> Thus there is "a language of truth, the tensionless and even silent depository of the ultimate secrets which all thought is concerned with" and this is "the true language" whose existence we assume unthinkingly as soon as we translate from one language into another. That is why Benjamin places at the center of his essay . . . the quotation from Mallarmé in which the spoken languages in their multiplicity and diversity suffocate, as it were, by virtue of their Babel-like tumult, the "*immortelle parole* [immortal word]," which cannot even be thought, . . . and thus prevent the voice of truth from being heard on earth with the force of material, tangible evidence. Whatever theoretical revisions Benjamin may subsequently have made in these theological-metaphysical convictions, his basic approach, decisive for all his literary studies, remained unchanged: not to investigate the utilitarian or communicative functions of linguistic creations, but to understand them in their crystallized and thus ultimately fragmentary form as intentionless and noncommunicative utterances of a "world essence." What else does this mean than that he understood language as an essentially poetic phenomenon? And this is precisely what the last sentence of the Mallarmé aphorism, which he does not quote, says in unequivocal clarity: . . . all this were true if poetry did not exist, the poem that philosophically makes good the defect of languages, is their superior complement.[59]

Notions of Language Growth, and Links Between Language Growth and Peace. The respective visions of Benjamin and Rosenzweig, those of "pure language" and of "one language," are not visions in the sense of dreams, of wishes, of faith alone, or of prescriptives for a rosy future dawn. They are descriptive of what each man discovered and confirmed about language in the act and in the process of translation. Their visions provide profound and linguistically concrete statements with regard to the facts and tensions of otherness evident in the multiplicities of language. To both men, peace, harmony among all human beings, is inherent, inheres in language, in each particular language, in seed.*

The notions of the "one language" and "pure language" for both are tied to and evidenced only in translation, but for Rosenzweig all speech is translation. In the act of translating, both Rosenzweig and Benjamin found themselves reaching down into the wells of their own language, and where the well seemed dry, a subterranean spring within their own language opened to them.

In a consideration of the notions of pure language and the one language as they occur throughout the two essays, it is soon apparent that the facets of Benjamin's "Task of the Translator" are not only more sharply cut but more highly polished than are those of Rosenzweig's afterword. The entire discussion for Benjamin's part can be restricted to his introduction to his Baudelaire book. Rosenzweig's after-

---

*"But those who finally came to be employed in the work as supervisors, even though it might be of the lowest rank, were truly worthy of their task. They were masons who had reflected much, and did not cease to reflect, on the building of the wall, men who with the first stone which they sank in the ground felt themselves a part of the wall. Masons of that kind, of course, had not only a desire to perform their work in the most thorough manner, but were also impatient to see the wall finished in its complete perfection" (*The Great Wall,* p. 74).

word needs to be set among several of his other writings in order to highlight what he only partially, or cursorily, states in the essay. The afterword refers at some length to medieval Hebrew poetry of Spain, to Hebrew and Arabic meters, and to other (interesting, but here irrelevant) technical aspects involved in translating. "The Task of the Translator" does not mention Baudelaire. Benjamin's essay easily stands alone; Rosenzweig's, only in excerpted fashion.[60]

Language growth means expansion, extension, and development from within a language. The growth of a language does not entail addition, absorption, or completion from without. Each language seed possesses within it potentiality for its own fullness of growth.

Yet each language, apart from Holy Scriptures, needs other languages in order that its own fullness of expression might be attained. Just as the seeds of various flowers variously require more or less sun and shade, more or less water, sandy soil or clay, and so on, for the seed to germinate and grow into the fullness of blooms, so too each language grows in accordance with external stimuli.[61] Insular languages, then, and peoples, and persons, have less of a chance to develop fully than internationally exposed ones. Individual languages spoken in cosmopolitan cities have the opportunity to develop richer tones and modes of expression than does a single language spoken in homogeneous small towns or ghettos. Whereas, however, the flower has no choice but to follow the laws of nature, language—national or personal—consistently exercises a choice to grow or not. The growing pains experienced by the language are such that sometimes ease, or the slothfulness of nongrowth is chosen.[62]

Sometimes the heinous imposition of not permitting language growth among a people is carried out, sometimes blatantly and cruelly, sometimes subtly. These language spirits, however, often live, while they need to, underground, vigilant for right conditions for rebirth and regrowth. Some indigenous peoples—languages—on the globe are currently experiencing painful regrowth.

What does it mean when the slothfulness of nongrowth is chosen? The tendency toward slothfulness of the powerful linguistic group, which sees no need to listen to inferior, lesser, poorer, weaker—that is, less expanded—linguistic groups, leads to a poisoned growth, a corruption on the part of the powerful group. The notion of Germanicizing—totalizing—all of Europe was already a dangerous sign, not only for others, but also for the dominating selves.

The powerful language, however, retains its richness, retains its fullness, even if that richness is a past, dead fact, and even if the lifefulness, that is, the continuance of life, is still actively vital only in the languages into which it has been translated. The original's life has undergone a change; its life lives in another language. A steady increase in translation of pre–World War II German philosophical works during the last two decades, especially on North American and French soil, is a strong case in point. Homer continued his life, not in Greek, but in Latin. As early as 1 October 1917 Rosenzweig had determined: "Translating is after all the actual goal of the mind [*Geistes*]; only when something is translated has it become really *audible,* no longer to be disposed of. Not until the Septuagint did revelation become entirely at home in the world, as long as Homer did not yet speak in

Latin he was not a fact. In a corresponding way, also translating from person to person."[63]

This idea corresponds to Benjamin's notion of the range
of life of an artwork being determined, not by nature, but
by history. In the afterlife of a work of art, Benjamin writes,
"which could not be called that if it were not a transforma-
tion and a renewal of something living—the original under-
goes a change."[64] This means that the original's growth
occurs in the translation. Thus the translating language necessarily must also grow, and therefore also undergo a change.

> For just as the tenor and the significance of the great works
> of literature undergo a complete transformation over the
> centuries, the mother tongue of the translator is transformed
> as well. While a poet's words endure in his own language,
> even the greatest translation is destined to become part of
> the growth of its own language and eventually to be ab-
> sorbed by its renewal. Translation is so far removed from
> being the sterile equation of two dead languages that of all
> literary forms it is the one charged with the special mission
> of watching over the maturing process of the original lan-
> guage and the birth pangs of its own.[65]

Benjamin speaks of translation as a literary form that is
charged with a mission: this mission is to express the truth
of divine revelation. "Translation keeps putting the hallowed
growth of languages to the test: How far removed is their
hidden meaning from revelation, how close can it be
brought by the knowledge of this remoteness?"*[66]

---

*"Now I have no wish whatever to represent this attitude as a
virtue; on the contrary. True, the essential responsibility for it lies

Rosenzweig speaks of the imperative of translation on personal and national levels. In a passage in "Die Schrift und Luther," written in 1926, Rosenzweig describes the resistance or slothfulness with regard to the imperative as "mad egoism." (The following emphasis of the especially pertinent two sentences is mine.)

> If then all speech is translation . . . , in speaking and listening, the "other" need not have my ears or my mouth—this would render unnecessary not only translation but also speaking and listening. And in the speaking and listening between nations, what is needed is neither a translation that is so far from being a translation as to be the original—this would eliminate the listening nation—nor one that is in effect a new original—this would eliminate the speaking nation. *These could be desired only by a mad egoism intent on satisfying its own personal or national life and yearning to be in a desert surrounded oasis. Such an attitude is utterly out of harmony in a world created to be not a wilderness but a place to contain every kind of people.*[67]

Thus, deliberate deafness to another's speech is that which detracts from healthiness in personal or national linguistic growth. The most beautiful words, terms, concepts can be corrupted, twisted, flattened, or otherwise effectively obliterated. A current example is the originally fine concept of

---

with the government, which in the most ancient empire in the world has not yet succeeded in developing, or has neglected to develop, the institution of the empire to such precision that its workings extend directly and unceasingly to the farthest frontiers of the land" (*The Great Wall,* p. 88).

"pluralism" which, fortunately, sheds the condescending, implicitly totalizing tenor and meaning of its precursor, the term "tolerance." The notion of pluralism coincides with one of the appellations of the "new thinking," the "and" philosophy. The word "and" safeguards against totalizing; it provides space between others, yet it links. The now degenerative derivative term "politically correct" carries overt tones of balance of powers in the word "politically," and of an unthinking, overly easy, trite rule-following, slogan-sounding, mathematical sense of right and wrong in the word "correct." The concept of "pluralism" is of course still actively, effectively addressed with passionate sincerity by sensitive theologians and philosophers, such as David Tracy and Michael Oppenheim, and with cautioning by Alain Finkielkraut.*

The concept of "pluralism," with its faith in the viability and transformative effectiveness of dialogue, is thereby directly linked to a notion of language as creative, and certainly to the notions of "pure" and "one" language of Benjamin and Rosenzweig. Their respective notions are explicitly nontotalizing: multiple languages can and do simultaneously speak the one language. Benjamin writes: "In the individual, unsupplemented languages, meaning is never

---

*"On the other hand, there is also involved a certain feebleness of faith and imaginative power on the part of the people, that prevents them from raising the empire out of its stagnation in Peking and clasping it in all its palpable living reality to their own breasts, which yet desire nothing better than but once to feel that touch and then to die" (*The Great Wall,* p. 88).

found in relative independence, as in individual words or sentences; rather, it is in a constant state of flux—until it is able to emerge as pure language from the harmony of all the various modes of intention. Until then, it remains hidden in the languages."[68]

The fact of the possibility of translation means to both Rosenzweig and Benjamin that a kinship among all languages must be presupposed. In the afterword Rosenzweig writes:

> the foreign poet calls into the new language not merely what he himself has to say, but rather he brings along with it the heritage of the whole language-spirit of his language to the new language, so that here a renewal of the language occurs not merely through the foreign person, but rather through the foreign language-spirit itself.
>
> That such a renewal of language through a foreign one is at all possible certainly presupposes that just as the language itself has given birth to each of its speakers, so too all human speaking [*Sprechen*], all foreign languages which ever were spoken and ever will be spoken, are contained in it in germcell at least. And that is the case. *There is only one language. There is no language trait of one language that does not evidence itself, at least in germ, in every other language.* [Emphasis added][69]

To Benjamin, the kinship of languages rests in the intention in each language toward pure language. The translator's task is "to release in his own language that pure language which is under the spell of another, to liberate the language imprisoned in a work in his re-creation of that work. For the sake of pure language he breaks through decayed barriers of his own language."[70]

The ultimate reason for translating, to Benjamin and Rosenzweig, is to fulfill the divine commandment that there shall be peace, that neighbor shall love neighbor, that the day of redemption might arrive. Rosenzweig writes: "Upon this essential oneness of all languages and upon the dependent commandment, namely that of universal human mutual understanding [*Verständigung*], is based the possibility as well as the task of translating, its Can, May and Shall. . . . [O]ne should translate so that the day of that harmony [*Eintracht*] of language, which can grow only in each individual language, not in the empty space 'between' them, may come."[71] Benjamin writes that although no translation is a permanent product like an artwork, nevertheless the goal of translation is "undeniably a final, conclusive, decisive stage of all linguistic creation," and points the way to the region of "the predestined, hitherto inaccessible realm of reconciliation and fulfilment of languages."[72]

With reference to Holy Scripture, and reminiscent of Rosenzweig's characterization of the Song of Songs as embodying the immediacy of language and revelation, Benjamin writes: "Where a text is identical with truth or dogma, where it is supposed to be 'the true language' in all its literalness and without the mediation of meaning, this text is unconditionally translatable."[73] Rosenzweig concurs with: "Among all books, the Bible is the one whose destiny is to be translated, and hence it is also the one translated the earliest and the most. . . . For while other translations always touch only a part of life, as a translation of Shakespeare only the theatre, a Bible translation engages in all spheres of life."[74]

"A real translation is transparent; it does not cover the

original, does not block its light," Benjamin claims, "but allows the pure language, as though reinforced by its own medium, to shine upon the original all the more fully."[75]

Rosenzweig agrees entirely: "[T]hese translations want to be nothing but translations. Not for a moment do they want to make the reader forget that he is reading poems not by me, but by Jehuda Halevi, and that Jehuda Halevi is neither a German poet nor a contemporary. . . . The translator makes himself the mouthpiece of the foreign voice, which he makes audible over the gulf of space or time."[76]

Where do the extendable borders of a growing, translating language stop? To Benjamin, the stop to the "bottomless depths of language" is "Holy Writ alone, in which meaning has ceased to be the watershed for the flow of language and the flow of revelation."[77]

Rosenzweig, too, holds that Scripture guides each language's growth on its translating path toward Truth. Even as wholly divine speech, Rosenzweig describes the Bible as being

> capable of chiming in with a tone which is foreign to it, which yet is a genuine human tone. . . . If the Bible did not have this hidden power to transform our errors into its truth, then it [translating] would be an even more hazardous enterprise than it already is. But that in itself is why the enterprise becomes imperative and a goal worthy of any effort. For this power of the Bible for transformation is the secret of its world-historical impact.*[78]

*"All the more remarkable is it that this very weakness [feebleness of faith] should seem to be one of the greatest unifying influ-

Conclusion

There is an end to language, then, an end to which it is translated. Created in the beginning as creature among creatures, it lives through and as Revelation. Its end is tensionless silence, a silence of peace. Walter Benjamin and Franz Rosenzweig feature among many who have spent much time, thought, energy, and experience in prolonged immersions in language use, theory, practice—and holiness. Like Aristotle's music of the heavenly spheres, pure language, always there, is often unattended, or heard, but not always consciously. Those who have pressed on with conscious, brave steps to delve for long whiles into the vast, unexplored caverns and to scale unclimbed majestic mountains of language have never yet reached the end of language. Those artists, poets, philosophers, speakers, those most sensitive of listeners, translators, all who try to expand language to express what has not yet been expressed in their own language, and succeed, can agree with Ludwig Wittgenstein, who on 17 December 1930 wrote the aphorism: "To run against the borders of language? Language is not a prison (Anrennen gegen die Grenze der Sprache? Die Sprache is ja kein Käfig)." No one has reached the outermost, and innermost,

---

ences among our people; indeed, if one may dare to use the expression, the very ground on which we live. To set about establishing a fundamental defect here would mean undermining not only our consciences, but, what is far worse, our feet. And for that reason I shall not proceed any further at this stage with my enquiry into these questions" (*The Great Wall*, p. 88).

borders of any spoken language, because its end is not yet. But dwellers in language reach and recognize, sometimes, a holy ground, a harmonious accord, that which is eternal. That which is eternal, unlike infinity, has borders, and can move, and be moved. Eternity, unlike infinity, can therefore be claimed to be and to have, order.

Language as Order

Northrop Frye, after decades of scholarly literary endeavors, came to characterize literature as "an order of words."[79]

To Karl Kraus, literature meant exclusively "linguistic form" [*Sprachgestaltung*]. He equated purity of language with purity of thought, and trusted that "the truth about mankind will occur to [sentences]."[80]

Of World War I he wrote: "What is at stake in the war is the life or death of language." To Kraus, as mentioned, language was an order of morality: "Because he considered language a direct index of morality, Kraus elevated it to man's essential concern, to which every other consideration should be subordinated. In its use of language he saw the cultural strength or weakness of a nation and the carrier of its spirit. Kraus firmly believed that purification of language would work to purify ethics."[81]

To Robert Musil, one's life must have a "narrative order" to make sense: "[T]he law of this life, for which one yearns . . . was none other than that of *narrative order*. . . . Lucky the man who can say 'when,' 'before' and 'after.'"[82]

The end of the order is not yet, but if we can trust the

holiness in the thought of Walter Benjamin and Franz Rosenzweig, then the acts of translating truths from artworks and elsewhere, from person to person, from nation to nation, inherently intend and strive toward order. Language, as a living order, itself helps those who take up the task of the translator.

2

Rosenzweig's Music Reviews

BARBARA E. GALLI

I shall proceed through three areas. First, I shall say a few words about Franz Rosenzweig as philosopher. I will do this as briefly as possible, for it will partially recapitulate some of chapter 1 but is needed to set the tone, as it were, for this chapter. Then I shall consider Rosenzweig's music reviews of 1928–29, which were written during the last year and a half of his life, in the final stages of amyotrophic lateral sclerosis, or what has come to be known as Lou Gehrig's disease, when Rosenzweig lay in a state of physical immobility and was unable to speak. He communicated these reviews as well as his other later writings by flickers of his eyelids, which his wife Edith understood and transcribed. I shall consider the reviews as follows: I shall state the always stimulating issues he raises, but leave all except one as unex-

Page number references to Rosenzweig's essay "The Concert Hall on the Phonograph Record" pertain to the translated English version of the essay that is published in this volume.

tended points. The extended point will cover the third area: Rosenzweig, in connection with the setting to music by Gustav Mahler (1860–1911) of poems by Friedrich Rückert (1788–1866), the *Kindertotenlieder* (Songs on the death of children), asks whether suffering may become beauty for us. To open toward an understanding of this question, we can look at other of Rosenzweig's writings, and attend to other songs and singers—here in particular the songs of the Sirens, set, as a song without words, in a fifty-two-word story by Franz Kafka, whom Rosenzweig admired. Let us have the story before us now, so that when we read it again later it will already sound familiar.

The Sirens

These are the seductive voices of the night; the Sirens, too, sang that way. It would be doing them an injustice to think that they wanted to seduce; they knew they had claws and sterile wombs, and they lamented this aloud. They could not help it if their laments sounded so beautiful.[1]

Principles of Franz Rosenzweig's Philosophy

Rosenzweig has been read as a romantic, a mystic, an existentialist, an idealist. Rosenzweig's self-designation for his system of philosophy is "absolute empiricism." By "absolute empiricism" Rosenzweig means that experience marks an absolute limit: we can *only* know *only* what experience teaches us. Within this scope of experience is included the human experience of being spoken to by God and of speaking to God.

How is Rosenzweig different from previous philosophers? The most striking feature is that he moves beyond reductionist systems that inevitably result in totalitarian worldviews. For Rosenzweig, as we shall see, there is not merely one essence to understand, but three, and, more importantly, the *relationships* among these three. Along with traditional, mainstream philosophy's primary inquiry, the question of essences, there was (and is), in contrast to Rosenweig's goal, a parallel quest to discover a single underlying essence.

Rosenzweig attempts a radical departure from tradition. He grants the success of the philosophical inquiry into the essences of world, God, and man through the antique, medieval, and modern periods respectively. At the same time he recognizes philosophy's repeated failure, and grave error, in believing multiplicities can be reduced to one element. Thales's famous position, for example, is that "All is water." In political realization, such reduction is totalitarianism. Rosenzweig, a philosopher emerging out of World War I, urged that a new philosophical question was needed if philosophy was to have any reason for continuing at all.

In order that philosophy reflect reality as it really is, Rosenzweig posits that reality cannot be reduced to a single element. There are, rather, three irreducible elements: world, God, and man. Out of philosophy's successful completion of the inquiry into essences, Rosenzweig determines a new beginning. The primary question concerning essences, What is? now becomes a question of relational event: What happens between the elements?

In order for the three elements to relate to one another, to learn truths about one another in drawing near and in drawing away in relationship, they need that truth-nourishing creation: time. Traditional philosophy had sought timeless truths; the new philosophy seeks truth in time. In Rosenzweig's system the categories of time across which truths are stretched are creation, revelation, and redemption. That is to say, world, God, and man relate to one another under the framework of creation, revelation, and redemption.

The organon for revelation and relation is language; and speech is a central concern for Rosenzweig's philosophy. Speech requires time. Mainstream philosophy holds speech to be an inadequate and faulty tool for formulations of truths and for communicating them. One of the names for the new philosophy is *Sprachdenken,* speech-thinking. Here, word, the act of speaking, and language, are common to both God and man. Full word for both God and man is word *and* response. Our cues for speaking come from someone other than ourselves. We speak until we understand one another. The ultimate end of speech—and language—is the wholeness, the peace, the harmony of silence, that coming to rest in shared silence. Ultimately there is only one language. Each individual language has in seed the capacity to understand fully every other language—through translating others' languages into one's own. *Languages* here means not merely, for example, French and English, but shared language between friends, enemies, men, women, and so on. If ultimately there will be peace, and if it is a commandment to make peace—Love your neighbor, then it is incumbent upon us to make our individual languages whole, through the efforts of listening and translating.

Rosenzweig's Insights into the Recordings

In these early moments of those huge technological waves, the Internet and the World Wide Web, circling around our globe, Rosenzweig's first point sounds especially striking. It concerns expansion and accessibility. In terms of space and time, he notes, the radio and phonograph record have "expanded the accessibility of the concert hall to an unforeseen extent." Though unforeseen, this expansion is the natural maturation of a historical development of the concert hall. Concert halls were introduced cautiously in the late eighteenth century, along with art museums. Peter Kivy, one of the few philosophers who concentrates on music, in his most recent book, of 1995, *Authenticities: Philosophical Reflections on Musical Performance,* calls the concert hall a "sonic museum."[2] The achievement of the museum—both sonic and art—prevails after the French Revolution and flourishes in the nineteenth century, that bourgeois century. This efflorescence does not result from political and social thrusts alone. Both Kivy and Rosenzweig observe that the Beethoven symphony required a great public hall, and both show that art works themselves are shaped according to this development of accessibility. Art is self-consciously created with its exhibiting method, place, or space in mind. But the audience, or viewers of the art are also influenced.

The year 1750 brought about the concert hall, which co-incided with the separation of chamber music and the symphony. Rosenzweig calls this the New Age; Kivy calls it "the great divide." For Rosenzweig, the unsurpassed monument of the new music is the last movement of Beethoven's Ninth Symphony.

Once the great divide, or the New Age arose, the audience for musical performance gathered in the sonic museum could no longer be a community or a closed circle of acquaintances. Instead, in the "colorful and chance combination" of such an audience, it became a representative of humanity. The audience combination can be *spatially* expanded "to the hundreds and thousands who share in the listening at the radio" and *temporally* expanded "to the future listeners of the phonograph record which was recorded at the performance." This expansion is only the legitimate conclusion of the public nature of the sonic museum—and its appropriate music: the symphony.

Chamber music, by contrast, although playable in the sonic museum, can never claim the concert hall as its home. Yet, by means of the concert hall, it too enjoys expansion. In an odd reversal, the phonograph record, which is a sonic reproduction of the public hall performances, opens chamber music, even to one who has no ability to play, "in ever-renewed listening . . . between his own four walls." For expert players, this of course affords a different kind of opening—and perhaps, unfortunately, also a kind of closing. On the ability to play music, Peter Kivy regrets the perpetual decline of amateur music-making (254). With the arrival of the recording industry, the *need* to play oneself in order to hear music disappears. Whereas Kivy expresses his regret, he nevertheless does assert that listening to classical music, in the sonic museum or at home on recordings, is "an intrinsic human good." Further, Kivy reveals the philosophical foundation of this good: the art and sonic museums are the practical embodiment of Kant's theory of aesthetics. This theory involves "a concept of an autonomous aesthetic experience, or aesthetic perception itself" accompanied by disinterested satisfaction: the contemplation of beauty. These museums, according to Kivy, constitute an aesthetic revolution, in which "all interactions with a work of art, except that of pure *contemplation,* became extraneous as well as destructive of the now favored 'aesthetic attitude'" (236). Let us recall this attitude when we discuss suffering and beauty: whether listening is an "intrinsic human good."

Concerning the mechanical as a medium for sound, or, from a different angle, the immediacy of sound at a remove, Rosenzweig compares the piano's clacking sound over the radio, its unyielding sound through a microphone, and its surprising suitability to phonograph recording. Still, there are those who "cannot get over the mechanical." In this issue of mechanical mediation Rosenzweig subordinates the medium to the art work itself. In his essay "The Concert Hall on the Phonograph Record," he writes

> In truth, as long as there is a certain, not too low, minimum quality of the reproduction, so if for instance in the case of the etching there is no autotyping and in the case of phonograph records no giving up of the gramophone horn, the work alone is the deciding factor. The same applies too to reproducing artists; here, too, the work alone is important, once certain minimum demands have been fulfilled. Beethoven remains Beethoven, even when the concertmaster of

the local orchestra is playing the violin, and kitsch remains
kitsch, even when Kreisler plays it. (see p. 123).

That is to say, Rosenzweig favors a sense of the invisibility
of the mechanical.

Christopher Hailey[3] concludes from research on music in
Weimar Germany that what the radio and phonograph records *claimed* they were delivering was far from what they
did deliver. Hailey compares the German experience of radio in the 1920s with the apparent invisibility of technical
mediation in the 1990s. He suggests that the technical medium is not truly invisibile but is "the result of a process by
which the human ear has redefined its needs and expecta-
tions to accommodate a new partner in the experience of
sound."[4]

Whereas Hailey is looking from the angle of sonic reception, Kivy investigates from that of aesthetics: "[I]s there any
aesthetic difference," he asks, "between a live performance of
a musical work and a perfect sound reproduction of it? Indeed, this is no longer a *Gedankenexperiment* but very close
to being a fait accompli, in the form of a compact disc"
(99–100). If contemplation of the "heard aesthetic" is the
aim of the sonic museum, then, Kivy concludes, "the real
sonic museum—its ultimate expression—is not the concert
hall but the perfect sound recording, where the visual has
been excised completely." I hasten to mention that this is
not Kivy's ultimate conclusion; his own argument runs otherwise, concluding that the visual *is* an integral part of performance practice, occasioned by the performing artist
through what Kivy calls "personal authenticity." This would

be evidenced, for instance, in the solo piano parts performed by Vladimir Horowitz. In "The Concert Hall on
the Phonograph Record," Rosenzweig also regrets the decline of "personal authenticity" in the face of imposing directions for playing engraved in the score, in what he calls
the "century of scientific editions" (see p. 135). Improvisation, "the essential distinctive mark of the art of virtuosity,"
"today seems to us so wrong, indeed nearly blasphemous,
that even the contemporary report that Beethoven, at the
first performance, had played his G-Major Concerto 'very
mischievously,' that is . . . with free flourishes, makes us
shudder slightly, as if to say: 'But is that allowed?'" (see
p. 135)

Neither Kivy nor Rosenzweig explicitly state this, but the
claim here for both seems to be that it is not technology
that is the source of worry, but rather an overly technical
human being who slavishly behaves according to rules instead of boldly and creatively acting.

The idea of sincerity, genuineness, of "personal authenticity" is especially interesting when considering the in-
volvement of the human voice, music with vocal parts. The
musical mass, and all the forms of liturgical music that flow-
ered by its side, Rosenzweig observes in "The Concert Hall
on the Phonograph Record", are the genuine descendants
of, and are of equal rank to, Attic tragedy (see pp. 124–25).

During the period of secularization of music through the
eighteenth century into the nineteenth, Rosenzweig detects
that even in sacred music there is a connection with the
"secular," "for genuine love of God cannot be expressed
differently from genuine earthly love—which we however

do not perceive for the earlier times, because from those times we consciously possess only sacred art" (see p. 126). The secularization of the centuries at times exhibits "a certain smooth excess of beauty" (see p. 127), more so in Felix Mendelssohn (1809–47) and less in Franz Schubert (1797–1828), but, in the opening movement of Auton Bruckner's (1824–96) *Te Deum,* there is "the comforting certainty that 'centuries' have no power over the relationship of the human being to God—because it not only depends on the human being, but also on God" (see p. 127).

The elements of speech are taken up also in his discussion of Haydn's *Creation,* now not only word and response but the communal "we," when with the Nineteenth Psalm, the "enchanted archangel solo voices [are] woven into the choir" (see p. 130). This weaving in of the solo voices is "more than a technical advance" and derives from "deeper reasons" (see p. 130). "The 'we' of the praying community supports itself by the hundredfold 'I' of its limbs, yet they can only say 'I' because the 'we' of the community carries it. This most intimate reciprocal interweaving of me and everyone now finds its form of expression" (see p. 130). The greatest expression of this interweaving, according to Rosenzweig, is Beethoven's *Missa Solemnis.*

In 1800 a new feature followed the separation of sacred and secular music: music of the spirit. This music flies over the world, but does not overcome it. This music of the spirit instead transforms the world (see p. 132). This music of the spirit "demands the concert hall as a space for its ringing out, just because it is a neutral space which is open to everyone. The prerequisite for the appearance of such a music is the unique encounter of a living philosophy with a living literature" (see p. 132). In Germany around 1800 this happened with Fichte, Schiller, Goethe, Hegel in Jena and Weimar. Musically, this is represented by the last movement of Beethoven's Ninth Symphony, that "unsurpassed monument."

"The final benefit of the sacred song, the combined singing of the I and the We now becomes the cradle of the newborn song of the spirit" (see p. 133). With the *sacred* song the basic form is that the voice frees itself from the choir. With the song of the *spirit,* the basic form is that the solo voice summons and awakens the choir.

It is precisely here that we come to the point of entry into the third area of discussing Rosenzweig's reviews, whose concern will be a sense of the song of the spirit. Only one recording, Rosenzweig writes, is available out of "the whole rich literature of the cantata-like musical compositions of classical-romantic world-literature and literature of life" (see p. 133): the setting to music (between 1901 and 1904) by Gustav Mahler's (1860–1911) of the five *Kindertotenlieder* by Rückert. "We don't even have," Rosenzweig writes, the exquisite compositions by Johannes Brahms (1833–97): the setting to music of *Harzreise im Winter,* the *Alto Rhapsody,* by Johann Wolfgang von Goethe (1749–1832); the Friedrich Schiller (1759–1805) "most beautiful poem" (18) *Die Nänie* (Song of lamentation); and *Hyperions Schicksalslied* (Song of destiny) by Hölderlin (1770–1892). All of these, Mahler's as well as Brahms's pieces here, are concerned, first, with loneliness and the accompanying sense of surrounding silence, and second, with a calling out either by the lonely one or by someone on behalf of the lonely one.

In the *Alto Rhapsody,* we have the lines "Die Öde verschlingt ihn./ Ach, wer heilet die Schmerzen" [The solitude devours him./ Ah, who can heal the pain]. The final stanza is a prayer beseeching God to play a note on His Book of Psalms that the lonely, embittered one will perceive and thereby be revived.

In *Die Nänie,* we have expression of that great romantic grief, the inevitable passing of beauty: all the gods and goddesses weep, that beauty must pass away, that the perfect must die.

In *Schicksalslied,* the Song of Destiny, we have the contrast of the gods wandering above in light, while the suffering human is flung from crag to crag from one hour to the next into the unknown.

In the *Kindertotenlieder,* we have the despairing lines "Das Unglück geschah nur mir allein!/ Die Sonne, sie scheinet allgemein!" [The misfortune has happened to me alone!/ The sun is shining for everyone!], followed by a sort of prayerlike tone: "Du mußt nicht die Nacht in dir verschränken,/ Mußt sie ins ew'ge Licht versenken!" [You must not fold the night in you,/ You must absorb it into the eternal light!]. Of this recording, which was sung by Rehkemper, the baritone from Munich, Rosenzweig writes: "The moving effect, even more moving in the silent despair than in the outbursts, extorts from the anxious heart of the listener the question that certainly confronts the questionability of all art and that we, were we only always really deeply moved would have to ask always: the question whether suffering—may become beauty for us" (see p. 134).

Suffering and Beauty—The Sirens as a Song of the Spirit

This century has brought a heightened quest to pose *right* questions concerning suffering. This quest, which wants to pose questions appropriately, with decorum, with a view to solution, must itself move through and dwell awhile within suffering. Neither the quest nor the question can be pleasurable, or indecorously beautiful. Two places where decorous attention to suffering is located are Kafka's writings and the Bible.

When he read Kafka's *Castle,* Rosenzweig observed in a letter of 25 May 1927 to Gertrud Oppenheim: "The people who wrote the Bible seem to have thought of God much the way Kafka did . . . and that is why reading it certainly cannot be called a pleasure."[5]

The question of suffering and beauty here can be posed through the fifty-two word story we have already encountered:

The Sirens

These are the seductive voices of the night; the Sirens, too, sang that way. It would be doing them an injustice to think that they wanted to seduce; they knew they had claws and sterile wombs, and they lamented this aloud. They could not help it if their laments sounded so beautiful.

A Sense of Questions Concerning Suffering and Beauty

In this story the Sirens suffer, but the beautiful form of their expression of it is not intentionally, self-consciously beautiful. Here suffering is not transformed: but instead, the suffering is formed beautifully. As with the events of suffering, and expressions of suffering in the Bible, here, too, action taken is not the avoidance of, but the facing of the event through literary expression. Here, as with, for instance, the Psalms, the literary is also musical expression.

There is a recurring, disturbing question concerning the permissibility of creating artworks that disclose—or is it cloak?—suffering in a beautiful form.

Borders of fields of inquiry are open, but let the search here lean on the philosophical. In the new thinking, we said, time nourishes knowledge and truths. In terms of time understood under a grammatical analysis of creation, revelation, and redemption, Rosenzweig interprets Genesis 1 as a narrative denoting past, representative of creation; the Song of Songs as imperative, denoting present, representative of revelation; and the Psalms of Praise 111–18, but especially 115, as choral language, denoting future, and representative of redemption. To Rosenzweig, moreover, these categories of time correspond to the three stages in the genesis of an artwork: creation is the stage of creator-artist; revelation is that of the artwork; redemption is that of the appreciative awareness of the spectator. So, to Rosenzweig, there is a connection between art, choral music or language, and redemption, or the end of all suffering.

We have moved into theological language, for at this

point—individual suffering, individual death—philosophy is inadequate. Rosenzweig is not of Plato's view that beauty is the mediator between the ideal and real worlds.[6] Art does not console. Rosenzweig is in closer kinship with Voltaire's view. Voltaire, with grave hostility, confronted the poet Alexander Pope (1688–1744). Pope's poetry, Voltaire sharply pointed out, aims at anaesthetizing pain by way of aestheticizing experience. Yet, the actual object of Voltaire's hostility was only partly the soothing of pain and the beautifying of events. More at issue was what Voltaire saw as the resultant political quietism.[7]

With regard to the experience of pain, in Voltaire we see the critique of art as opiate, as that which can deaden the senses of pain, and therefore also suppress or deter otherwise possible redresses to certain evils. While the perceived and expressed experience of the suffering is altered through a distorting form and formulation, the existence of the suffering, though perhaps now unfelt, persists, underneath the anaesthesia. The suffering, though unperceived, itself does not in reality change. Thus, this kind of aestheticization cannot be in the service of truth and reality.[8]

If Rosenzweig has any affiliation with romanticism, it is certainly not in this area. Suffering itself never is pleasurable for him. Art is not a consolation in this sense either.

With Kafka's story, ultimately a larger truth surfaces, which I can open only slightly here. It is not the sufferers themselves, not the Sirens, who are affected by their own beauty of expression. Here, within the story, the ones who are anaesthetized are the ones who observe—hear—the suffering of these others. The observers within the story, that is, are desensitized to these others' sufferings, and attend to the Sirens only because they sound beautiful. Those allured by the Sirens, therefore, are falsely allured. In Kafka's story, no blame lies anywhere, neither in the viewers nor in the Sirens, and it is a sad story of suffering, unpleasant, but beautiful. And yet those of us who observe—or imagine hearing—the Sirens through Kafka's description from outside the story, must be moved to draw near to the Sirens in compassion for their suffering—not for their beauty—even though we know that those who draw near will surely suffer too.

A Sense of the Answer

In his afterword to his translations of poems by Jehuda Halevi,[9] Rosenzweig writes of repeated reactivation of poems and songs, in reading them, in liturgically reciting them, or, we might add, possibly in playing them as recordings. Rosenzweig writes that

in the final analysis *repetition* is altogether the great and *only form which man has for expressing what is entirely true for him.* In these poems one can encounter the always renewed words of humility and devotion, *of despair and of trust in redemption,* of world-aversion and longing for God, of repentance of sins and of faith in mercy—one can encounter this, but one does not thereby remove the fact from the world that the heart of the poet and *the hearts of those for whom he has composed are full of these feelings and demand expression for them.* The lie has many possibilities, the truth only a few, at base always only one. The fact that truth does not become tired of saying anew this always One again and again testifies to its enduring power. In the mouth of the lover the word of love never becomes old, the word which from the mouth that shams love already withers when it is spoken for the first time. (183)

Note especially here Rosenzweig's coupling of the themes "of despair and of trust in redemption," and with that let us move on now to the possibility that in the despairing cry of complaint, lament, yearning, to God, and even in the despair of being heard or of receiving a response, that this despair is already a prayer, on the brink of praise. For there is a point beyond despair: deathly silence in life or after, when the dead cannot praise God.

In speech, the only way to become a choral or communal "we" is through at least two audible "I"s. The artwork cannot be an "I." Psalm 115 is the sole place in the Psalms where idol worship, the prophetic theme, is raised. The idols are regarded as art works.[10] The idols, like art detached from life, are ridiculed, because in them "the life of divine love is said to petrify into inaction and speechlessness."[11] The communal praise God, however, in the trust that the "we" who praise now will one day become and be a "we" that includes everyone, "we all." "Not the dead," sings the Psalm, "*but we,* we will praise God from this time forth and to eternity." Rosenzweig emphasizes "the conquering But," the "But we are eternal." This "we" that praises in the immediacy of the now of life, conquers death because it is "this triumphal shout of eternity. Life becomes immortal in redemption's eternal hymn of praise."[12]

Praise out of suffering can emerge only when death is fully feared and faced. This can be aided by the arts and by liturgy. Traditional Western philosophy teaches, however, *denial* of death, denial even of the *fear* of death.[13]

A Clearer Answer

In a lecture series entitled "Faith and Knowledge,"[14] an either-or juxtaposition is raised in a discussion of art: either ideal (art) or life (view). And within this juxtaposition Rosenzweig contrasts the gesture in the art world and the genuine gesture in life. A gesture in life involves immediacy, and for a fleeting moment it dissolves space and time between two people. Or, as Schelling would put it, it involves indifference in the sense of nondifference: collapse of distance and time between finite and infinite. This can happen with a glance. "A word forgets itself and is to be forgotten; it wants to perish in the answer. The power of the glance, however, does not perish with the moment. Once an eye has glanced at us, it will glance at us as long as we live."[15] In the art world, such a glance is not possible either in the fine arts, which creates its "pure" space, or in music which creates its pure time. Such a glance is possible only in poetry, which is beyond space and time, and instead lives in its element: thought, idea, conception. Rosenzweig writes in the *Star* that only as book is poetry "truly 'pure' art; it is in its pure world of ideas there, each work in its own one. . . . The very act of reading it aloud [however] already forces it out of this pure world of its imagination and makes it somehow common."[16]

How can this eternity really be sensed as *present* in life? Rosenzweig writes: "Only he who has the future [of redemption] as reality *media in vita,* who has learned to die at any moment . . . , only he *is alive.* . . . But to learn this is a difficult art and costs much strength and pains. Nobody gets it for free. We can all only pray that the strength for these pains be given to us and does not run out. Amen."[17] For such strength all we can do is pray. The great deeds, those that live beyond us, and the strength for these deeds do not happen through "willing" them, nor when one wills them. To pray is to await the unforeseen.

"Only by prayer can we get to every deed, every true deed, not by splitting hairs, not by devising" (115). "The deed is not the work of a 'freedom,' morality . . . rather the fulfillment of a prayer" (115). And: "There is no unfulfilled prayer" (116).

In each deed, according to Rosenzweig, the human being can prove "whether he has learned from life to be free in life, in each deed he can prove whether life has taught him—how to die" (117). If not for the arts, the kingdom of ideals would *really* be a kingdom of shadows. That is, only the arts—the thought world—open up, and depict the hidden ideal world. Here, then, the world of thought, of the ideal, needs that which faith holds suspect: the form, which is always in danger of becoming an idol. No images are permitted, no definitions, no limits. The particular human being, Rosenzweig claims, lives for the sake of a single gesture, a gesture that is so individual that he cannot talk about it. It is the gesture that most often occurs with "the death of a near one," a gesture of love, expressed, for example, in the *Kindertotenlieder.* The need to talk about this gesture necessitates the artform. For the sake of this gesture, Rosenzweig claims, we need forms, and continually, because "of them, one can speak at any rate" (119). "Art is the assistant," Rosenzweig writes, "it transmits" (119). "Art . . . is not an ideal at all, but rather a—surrogate (or at any rate an aid) for life" (119).

Then, to the question whether, as Plato suggested, beauty perhaps forms the *bridge* between ideal and life? Rosenzweig replies: "Beauty blooms only in song. Beauty belongs wholly to the 'kingdom of shadows,' is *more visible* only as distinguished from the other shadows" (118).

Rosenzweig characterizes love, not as an abiding attribute or attitude, but as an event that is experienced anew again and again. Beauty, too, for Rosenzweig, is an event and not a static fact. Past art, however, Rosenzweig notes, is *not* dead; past life *is* dead. Still, "the forms of life," he insists, "have to be *living* forms,—*aut non sunt*. (Art must be nearer to life or farther from life, but it must be *beautiful*.) The gesture of life may be more beautiful or less beautiful, but— it must be *living* ('genuine')" (118).

There are two dangers in the process of transmission of the gesture by artworks. These are the same dangers inherent in education. The artwork first makes room for this gesture in one's life, it prepares one for it; and then the artwork incorporates this gesture and preserves it. Both the preparation and the preservation are "very dangerous. The first, because it eventually blocks the way of the gesture, the second, because it eventually trivializes it" (120).

Reactivating artworks reactivates the living gesture, and "the [living] gesture is victorious again and again over both dangers. For it is fed out of inexhaustible life" (12). "Art must become rigid (only *l'art pour l'art*) only when it wants to escape this rule of the *living* gesture, or even to rule over *it*" (120).

"For we are not supposed to 'flee' 'from the narrow, stifling life into the realm of ideals.' We are not supposed to flee at all. We are supposed to live. Better 'narrow and stifling,' but *real,* than 'wide and free,' but *ideal.* The alternative is: ideal or life. But the flight into the ideal is forbidden. Thus only life remains."[18]

Fair Forms of Beauty

We could not properly formulate the question. Recently Alan Udoff raised the notion that Logos—word—can be understood as divided between question and praise. To question God (or anyone) is to distance Him. In praising God, God comes to presence. When all power of willing has become futile, and when suffering is such that praise seems impossible and precluded, then the expression of a lament, of sung or spoken despair, can be nothing other than the edge of prayer, a prayer for a gesture, for presence of another. The lament makes room for that other.

To Kafka, as we know, writing is a form of prayer. Part of the pain in the story of the Sirens is that we, and they, are not sure to whom they are lamenting, and they have not yet received their answer to their beautiful laments.

3

Franz Rosenzweig
A Commemorative Writing

VIKTOR VON WEIZSÄCKER

I may call Franz Rosenzweig a fellow-student and a friend from youth.[1] I see him in front of me in a skiing outfit in the Black Forest, in the bar, as a Freiburg medical student. Shortly before his pre-medical examination he confessed to me there that he would switch over now to history, for he had chosen medicine only in order not to debase to the everyday that which he cherished most; he had understood that that had been childish. He also put aside the violin as a youth because (he intimated to me) the revelatory music could have carried him away too far. But when he switched over from medicine to philosophy and history, certainly his innermost domain was already filled, instead of with these

"Franz Rosenzweig: Eine Gedenkschrift" was written by Viktor von Weizsäcker (1886–1957) in 1930 and appears in *Gesammelte Schriften: 1. Natur und Geist: Begegnungen und Entscheidungen* (Frankfurt am Main: Suhrkamp Verlag, 1986), pp. 413–14.

sciences, with another, more secret content. A secret forced him thus always to the making of masks; this detachment from the world around, I dare claim, lay hidden in every utterance, even the most decisive one of his later, heroic years. Then the mental essence of the young scholar, which he really was at that time, extended to great fateful proportions. Sarcasm and probing skepticism transformed knowledge, cognition, belief to mere symbols. The deeper the shaft was driven into what was the dark and hard and hardest, the higher towered the edifice of relative layers of meaning, which were not cast off, in order to make things easier for oneself, but which one instead bears in order to test and steel one's power. Rosenzweig remained a fighter; he fought not for "what was right" [*die gute Sache*], but with the living opponents that we have in our own breasts. I believe he enjoyed the proud and elegant armed combat with himself, which men win who have a piece of the world in themselves. When he could still get about in the outdoors, he carried his breast arched forward and his head stretched back with his chin lowered. Capriccio and scherzo surrounded the solemn movement and bent the upward swing of the soul like a blade back to the reality of the being born and bound here and in this way, to the tense irony of existence. When I try to speak with Franz Rosenzweig after his death, the gesture which he makes toward me remains as always restrained and serene. I shall always understand the hint and never permit myself the encroachment of interpretation. That which was visible of him is now fulfilled. His secret is the eternal bridge that made him [who was] faithful to ties that were strange to me, my eternal friend.

PART TWO

Franz Rosenzweig's Writings

4

Hic et Ubique!

A Word to Readers and Other People

Hic et ubique—
Let us shift our ground![1]
Hamlet, 1.5

Before the War the German publishing system was wasting away from the same illness as were all other creatures: over-feeding. This is the actual sin of what today one brands with rash and little thought-out judgment as the "capitalist system." The sources of this overfeeding flow on all sides. The publishing houses and also the codependent printer's suffered almost—it sounds almost legendary today—from a "hunger for manuscripts." The public, on the other hand, at

Written in 1919 in Cassel as a memorandum to the planned establishment of the "Neubau-Verlag." Appeared in *Kleinere Schriften,* 1937, and in *Zweistromland,* 1984, pages 413–21. Of the three publishers, a "pagan," a Jewish, and a Christian, only the last one, the Patmos Verlag, was realized.

least if one trusts the lists of new releases, seemed to be obsessed with a real craze for reading. In future centuries it would be an amusing and rewarding task for cultural-historical doctoral candidates (if this species of people really still survive the present generation) to establish how many readers would have had to have read how many hours daily in order to polish off everything that was being printed; a calculation of one copy of a printed work per reader, which in the land of lending libraries and book lenders would be calculated very modestly, would yield a number of the population with which Germany would have come out of the last war differently than is the case. Unless such a people of readers, in spite of their majority, would have done even worse than the actual German people, who, although of a lesser number, are fortunately not so glutted by reading.

But let us be satisfied: those oceans of books were intended to be actually exhausted by the reader. In the end the book does not possess any magical powers that could compel the harmless passerby to become a reader. No book opens itself; he who opens it and leafs through it after all has to attribute this to himself. So if this ocean was not intended to be emptied, then perhaps to be swum through. It was probably enough if these books found only owners instead of readers. And really, the great magician capitalism brought this about: it was obviously able to force for its products, if not readers, then buyers. How could it otherwise be explained that almost all great works of world literature before the War surged into the market not in one new printing, no, in two, three, and multiple new printings? A certain self-contemplation already began here before the War and

determined a portion of the publishing houses, to put together their separately undertaken editions of the classics in
a single one. On the whole, however, the witches' sabbath
of capital raged on. That artificial production of needs, its
universal hallmark, drove itself further, a wheel constantly
rolling forward by its own weight.

Then came the War. He who could have expected that it
would set a goal to the mad movement, would have—here
as everywhere—been mistaken. The War did not bring—
here as everywhere—an end to capitalist commerce, it only
shifted its territory. The great slogan that it produced for
commercial life was—here as everywhere—reorientation.
In place of "industry and commerce" of peacetime there
came that of wartime. Really "industry and commerce" in
the sense of Hamlet's words to Horatio. The baking from
the funeral meal of peace made cold dishes for the marriage
feast of the dead.[2] Among what now emerged, little was
worth talking about. The War's effect on the intellectual
[*geistig*] life, which people had hoped for at the beginning,
could be felt less and less as "fiction" and "scientific" war
literature piled up higher. Instead of this what was old was
pushed onto the market in endless quantities and in packag-
ing that became more and more field gray in warmed up
and in cold dishes. What did it matter that this market now
had extended deep into Flanders, Macedonia, Estonia? It
was the same artificial creation of need, and the same artificial satisfaction. The wheel of capitalism rolled on, even
though its former golden spokes were now wrapped in paper. Then the collapse came.

And now things had to change. The pedestal under the

feet of Mammon foundered, the idol to whom in military disguise even the last five and a half years had paid homage. No new heart will grow by itself in the stony breast of this idol. For he doesn't have one. But when the ground beneath him sank away, he had to break apart crashing down and make room for more human forms. Had to. But it seems that even Mammon, though not a human being, does not have to be compelled.[3] Even today, a year later, he is making no move to fall. Again, as everywhere, in the book trade also it looks actually as if nothing had happened. Or no, some things have changed. The cheap, indeed even the inexpensive book has almost disappeared. But the luxury book is experiencing, so it seems, its high point for the first time. And the production throws itself onto this territory with almost an even heightened lack of unconsciousness. Like everyone in the country, so, too, the book trade celebrates its dance festivals at the edge of the volcano that had hardly come to rest and threatened a new eruption at any moment. The Flood is already here. But humanity staggers as if it were still permitted to say "après nous" [after us]. It does not want to admit it.

Healing can always only come, here in this individual territory as everywhere, from those who want to admit it. It is no help—here as everywhere!—to behave as if nothing had happened. One does not escape despair [*Verzweiflung*] in the long run by suppressing the doubts [*Zweifel*] in the permanence of what still only just persists. He who does not have the courage to go through the bath of steel of despair, his hands are no use for building anew. And building anew is necessary. Building anew, however—this does not mean a thoughtless carrying on of the activity, even less does it mean putting makeup on corpses. To building anew there belongs a determined tearing down of what was old, clearing away the rubble that might only find use as bricks for the new building; and once that tearing down and clearing away has been accomplished, then a new plan and new builders—here as everywhere.

Here as everywhere—but what does it mean: "here"? For the "here" is what concerns us, must concern us—here as everywhere! Should we then entirely and fundamentally break with the capitalist usages? Yes, we should. A small shelter in the meantime may be left to them in the luxury editions and similar camp followers of the old system; here also, a little policy of tax expropriation may run alongside the actual "socialization," and as such the luxury edition may lighten the still always overfull moneybag of the new-rich or old-rich amateur. But apart from this small time-conditioned inconsequence, it is a matter of putting the entire publishing business on a new foundation as far as it does not, by immediate dependence on practical needs, still have the golden basis of craftsmanship.[4] Where this new foundation is to be looked for is not hard to say: precisely in the craftsmanship and its golden basis. This is what the publishing house has, which placed itself directly into the service of definite, practical goals; it knows for whom it works; it knows its customers; it works by subscription. What the committed publishing house already has, that is precisely what the hitherto free one needs.

For it does not at all change the capitalist system, if in place of the capitalism till now of publishers there emerges a capitalism of authors, as is for instance desired by the Association for the Protection of German Writers. It is not because "the other" is its beneficiary and not "I" that the capitalist system is destructive. This is the innermost weakness of the present radical change, as of any radical change, that its representatives in their hearts were not of a very different mind; like that old slave who when set free was given money, and, to the question as to what he was going to do now, replied: to buy a slave. No, capitalism is to be condemned just like slavery as a system, independent of its representatives; just as it also just like slavery can in single cases establish quite irreproachable relationships. It is important, then, to replace it as a system. And the path of this replacement can only be the way back from the free, unrestrained market production to the committed, subscribed customer production. The "pure spirit" [*Geist*] yearns for a body; from being airily free from purpose and charge, it yearns for a restriction, it is tired of being shown like a dancing bear in the marketplaces by the roving Mammon to a curious rabble that comes and goes; it demands honest work with a master who needs it and who guarantees it shelter and livelihood—no less, but also no more. The publishing house should be a middleman for it between itself and a "circle of customers"—its "circle of customers."

So then the publishing house with a definite "direction"? But haven't we had that for a long time already? Leaving aside for the moment the publishing houses that are not confessionally determined, are not the publishing houses that grew large in the twenty years before the war all more or less servants of a clearly marked direction? What is new about it? What reason is there to make a lot of words, when after all nothing more is to be promised than what we already have? Not so fast, that's not how it is. True, the large pre-War publishing houses did take on intellectual directions, who could doubt it? From the naturalism of S. Fischer to the aestheticism of Insel and on to the Hieratismus of the Pages for the Arts, from the Religion of Culture of Diederich to the Activist Revolution of K. Wolff—none of the reigning trends of the German intellectual life [*Geistesleben*][5] seems to be unrepresented. It does not merely seem so, it is so. But what is needed is precisely not a representation of "intellectual trends." "Intellectual trends"—on the contrary, it is in this concept that the whole lie of the capitalist age hides, carrying its dagger under the cloak of the "mind" [*"Geist"*].[6] For the true life of the mind knows no "trends." Trends flow above the unchanging river of life, apparently churning it up, in truth only just moving it. Only movement, not—creation. That which is constant is moved, that which is silent is prattled away and spoiled by noise, but in every trend and noisy movement people remain what they always were. The trend that passes over them is only superficial. There are no creatures more alike than the "intellectual ones" [*geistig*] because they are only moved intellectually, not created out of the mind [*Geist*]. That which is created by the mind would have to both mentally and bodily [*geistleiblich*] give evidence of the mind [*Geist*] that created it. That which is moved by the mind shows only the movement that flows above it, at best through it. The swords may be crossed, the words of faith may fight each other, but the uncanny family resemblance of the faces gives the lie to the enmity of hands and tongues. It is not the case that we are speaking of bodies out of the spirit [*Geist*] still differentiated through differently created countenances, even in moments when they clasp hands in reconciliation. We are speaking here rather of a mass, undifferentiated in itself and indistinguishable because it is undecided, which only wants to be "moved," only "flowed through," only "animated." It is just from the intellectual ones [*Geistigen*] that movements, tendencies, animations are lured, which awaken the appearance of the distinguishable life forms in the chaos of undecidedness.

Which is the magic that pours the appearance of movement over these masses? Where does the magician sit? It is the same one who in commercial life hurled into the chaos of a mass, torn from the naturalness of need, the endless artificiality of the "essential commodity" and thus falsified need into addiction, necessity into frenzy, way of life into fashion—it is the capitalist spirit. The same which, only intellectually [*geistig*] disguised, who hurled here the arbitrary, flighty words of its "mottoes" into the tumult of the detached individualities and collected those who had fallen out of the bonds of the natural conscription of the spirit [*Geist*] into groups of mercenaries who were brought together only through the magic of the name of the leader or the glamour of the uniform. Thus necessarily all ailments of commercial capitalism had also to afflict this, his intellectual brother. In intellectual life just as in commercial life—here as everywhere!—the ailments of the lack of restraint, of the lack of content and artificial fulfillment of the satisfaction of the need (which was created for the purpose of being satisfied) in a nutshell: the lack of belief in the creation and its replacement through the "creative." And that is why here as there the same single path of possible healing is this: looking for the circles in which the natural bloodstream of the mind still circulated, and fitting production into the service of these circles. But which ones are they? Where is the spirit [Geist] still at home today, instead of wandering naked and bare about the streets, in houses that are finished, dilapidated though they may be? For only where one is accustomed to domestic life, only there, genuine and founded need for building anew can grow.

Where is the spirit still at home? Neither trade, nor guilds, nor the family, nor science, nor art still had a spirit of its own in the past century. The year 1789 drove out the established domestic spirits that had already become restless and no longer felt comfortable within their old four walls. They had all, insofar as they wanted to belong to this world, fled under the one great protective roof that had remained and that now, when it remained as the only one, had become widely visible: that of the state and of its national culture. All spirit was "national spirit" [Volksgeist], the nation had become the domicile of the spirit, or more exactly, the nations. Only one kind of spirit [Geist] still ensured its own domicile beside the nations, the spirit of religion that is essentially independent of the nation [Nebenvölklich]. But as the culture, which before 1789 was still universally Western, had now become a multitude of national cultures, so the spirit of Christianity, which earlier, in spite of the division of beliefs, at any rate was Western in common, in the nineteenth century sought its refuge in "confessions." Both

Protestantism and Catholicism unconsciously renounced their universal right and organized themselves, instead of as Church rather into what actually were enormously extended sects, that is, the confessions. Judaism also, entering the Western arena in 1789 after centuries of encapsulation, obediently followed the command of the hour and became confession.

The cultural as well as the religious forces thus renounced their proud right to be all-embracing life forces and limited themselves to mere partial powers. There was no longer a European language; the good European who was still a matter of course in [Gottfried Wilhelm] Leibniz [1646–1716], Voltaire [1694–1788], and even still in [Johann Wolfgang] Goethe [1749–1832], became in the nineteenth century the fantastic claim of an eccentrically lonely brain; the European did not want to be addressed as European. He did not want to be a "human being" [*Mensch*]; this word lost its boldly pagan sound, the patent of nobility that stemmed from the day of creation that it had possessed in the eighteenth century; instead of being addressed as a human being the European wanted to be addressed only as a German, a Frenchman, that is, only as the nationally characterized portion of his being. He did not want to be entirely domiciled, but rather to keep to himself something that was without a home, something that was purely personal. The designation German, which encompassed only one part of his humanity, was guaranteed for him by such a reservation of the personal aspect more than the all-embracing designation human being. The readiness to associate as full human being with the literary public, as the great men of the eighteenth century still did, a [Jean Jacques] Rousseau [1712–88], a [Gotthold Ephraim] Lessing [1729–81], even a [Friedrich] Schiller [1759–1805], got lost almost without a trace in the nineteenth century. In the same way now even the Christian or Jew did not want to be addressed as Christian or Jew. His Christianity or Judaism became for him a mere partial concern, he had Christian or Jewish "interests"; true, he demanded a literature that was directed at these interests; but he refused to have to be Christian or Jew, addressed wholly as Christian or Jew, as a thinker, an artist, a politician. He actually had no desire for it. Just as the "religious aspect" was allowed to become a partial region of culture for the national-cultural human being, so on the other hand the Christian or Jew saw nothing wrong in abandoning himself to a "culture" that was hostile to the forces of his revelation, as soon as he stepped out of the inviolable precincts of his faith. The "national being" had forgotten that nationalism is nothing more (and also may be nothing more according to its deepest meaning) than that of which it is—ethnicism!—the literal translation: paganism. And the "religious being" had forgotten that faith is nothing if it does not want to be everything; and that the human being can only believe when he "lives—in his belief."

The collapse of Europe deflated [*entgeistet*] both nationalism and confessionalism. What remains are empty husks, the mere Ism: nationalism without nation, confessionalism without confession. The spirits most at home in them have once again become homeless. And thus they are now seeking a new permanent place. The old bonds had to become fetters for the human being, precisely because they wanted to bind him not in his entirety, but only partly; for it is such bonds alone that bind the whole human being, change from fetters to a dress, in which he moves freely once he has put it on and has become used to it. Freed from those partial bonds, whose claims the human being may no longer acknowledge just because they are too undemanding, he now feels confronted by decisive questions, which concern him as a whole. Time asks the human beings of today nothing less than: Who are you? Who do you want to be? You as a whole human being, not in one part of your being? and in being so asked, he senses how already the answer to these questions lies prepared which had only remained mute till now because no one asked the question. Thus it happens that human beings today are separated into three masses, which in distinction from earlier on are definitely not merely intellectual "tendencies" or merely unintellectual "interest groups" but rather each one of which includes both: "intellectual" and "unintellectual"; for they are more than mere "tendencies" and "groupings" of a "human material" basically similar, but rather are basically different human communities. A community between human beings emerges everywhere only where human beings came together as a whole, already in itself each a "community" of manifold powers and gifts. Indeed, this total commitment of the separate individual, this inter-personal community, is so very much the characteristic of all genuine inter-human community that it even establishes as a silent sign the secret alliance of those who refused any community and want to be separate individuals. If they only really want to be so entirely, if they sincerely spurn letting themselves be finally absorbed into any partial bonds, then they form in their apparent and desired incompatibility a community, just as evolved, just as real, as the communities of those who want to have everything in common with each other.

So today the question, Who are you? is posed to every individual, and just by being focused on, the you, but the whole of it, organizes human beings into big masses and forces each one to profess his faith with a definiteness that was unheard of earlier on. Today one after the other is beginning to discover who he is: Christian, Jew, pagan speak their loud and decisive: "This is what I am," which had not been heard for a long time. And because each of them becomes conscious of being able to be totally what he is, or not at all, so each of these three masses begins to form a closed circle, which in itself must drive forth out of the roots of his faith, or lack of faith, a whole tree of life, or the root itself will dry up for him. In their Hic it is necessary for all of them to find the Ubique.

With this the basis is given for a reconstruction of the publishing system. For here if anywhere we have today the natural circles to which production as customers has to adjust itself, in order to feel the ground under their feet again. Author and publisher have to know whom to address first. This does not exclude that the three circles supplement one another again, further also does not exclude that the individual is "interested" also in that which the other circle includes, but yet always interested as in something that does not belong to himself directly, is not "written for him." For it must come to this that books are again "written for particular bodies"; all books have all too long been written only for the spirit. A little counterbalance is needed. Only out of the balance of body and mind does the soul rise up.

When in this way again embodied spiritual [*geistig*] communities stand facing the writer, or better, when the writer feels in his writings as an authorized member of such living bodies, then the publisher will naturally recover his health again, having become a servant instead of the lord of literature that he used to be in the capitalist age. It is here as everywhere: the strong heavenly wind of necessity must fill the flags of time fluttering here and there, capriciously changing with every breath of wind, so that they proudly billow out again and may stride at the head of the advancing armies. Necessity, under which each flock gathered singly, may and should then also reunite the separated armies to a common work. Above the Christians, Jews, pagans, as they are herded together in the pen of Germany, around which the civilized wolves of the whole cultural world are howling today, above them all there hangs a common need, there hangs beside the individual necessity, which can only be satisfied by each community in its own lap, the common necessity of reconstruction; the three reconstructed publishing houses will serve this common necessity together, regardless of the special work of each single one. But incidentally let each one find in his Hic, in the point where he is standing, his standpoint, his all, his Ubique. Enough time and strength have been wasted with bad blending, with extrinsic combinations of what cannot be combined, with a tolerance, before which the created and developed differences became blurred in a fog of emptiness of thought and feeling. Long enough did the individual believe he had to devote himself to "tendencies" [*Richtungen*] at the cost of his natural wholeness, in order to become instead of a focused one [*Gerichteter*], someone who focuses [*sich Richtender*] on anything. Long enough did the motto of the times say: orientation, whether old or new—and orientation means after all a focusing [*Sichrichten*]; he who is focused does not first have to orient himself. Long enough had Nathan's word about the love that everyone should emulate for himself, been changed according to the spirit of the times to a lovelessness, though free of "prejudices," and to indifference of everyone toward everyone. Nobody sensed any longer that truth is an "ancient coin that had been weighed" and not a little find that the uprooted and unspiritual individual may arbitrarily gather together out of all present and past treasure chests.

The fable of the three rings had lost the meaning that its creator had given it. Let us renew the dusty symbol. Let us not shrink from again erecting, each of us, on our Hic, the new building of his Ubique. The specter of the slain epoch itself exhorts us from the grave-studded earth to swear on the sword of its young, innocent successor and heir who has come, to set right again that which had been put out of joint. Let us shift our ground!

5

"Fighters"

The publishing house *Frommann* (H. Kurtz) and Prof. *Hans Ehrenberg*[1] are bringing out in five enticing little volumes the first series of a "philosophical paperback library," which represents something entirely new in the philosophic-historical book market. They are neither mere editions nor mere representations, but rather the publisher has found a highly promising new way. In each case five selected texts are introduced by five editors as congenial as possible to the text, and the general editor has to play the discreet but decisive role of a good seminar leader: it is he who determined the topic of the exercise, and divided the "seminar papers" for the individual classes among the most suitable speakers (every seminar leader knows that the most suitable ones are

---

"Kämpfer," written in the spring of 1923, appeared in the newspaper *Die Arbeitsgemeinschaft,* the periodical for the concerns of adult education classes, and whose editors were Dr. Robert von Erdberg, Prof. Dr. A. H. Hoffmann, Dr. Werner Picht. It was reprinted in *Kleinere Schriften,* 1937 and in *Zweistromland,* 1984, pages 423–25.

always those who volunteer for a theme when the leader makes known the list of topics in the first classes); now his further task consists essentially in the appropriate order of the five classes and perhaps occasionally in taking over himself one or the other of the seminar papers. Thus the student is given what he needs: independent knowledge of the sources, a personal, stimulating, and exciting introduction into each individual one, and the soft but sure hand of the experienced master who, instead of teaching him dogmatically by guiding him from source to source, sends him on the only way that leads to the goal of the philosophical "education" that in itself is questionable but yet always enticing: the path of one's own experience of thinking. He who knows this, and he who knows how difficult it is for the individual to follow this pathway today without guidance, and he who knows how much more than ever the student is in danger of swearing blindly in *verba magistri* [the words of the teacher]—and mostly what kind of a *magister* [teacher]!— he will hardly know how to save himself in this time when the aged universities and the young high schools, which unfortunately are mostly more precocious than truly young, can barely cope with a multitude in need of philosophy. He will greet the Frommann Paperback Library as an attempt at the education toward thinking for oneself—"education" and "thinking for oneself": an incompatibility that *must* be reconciled.

The first group on hand poses the topic: *Fighters.* It becomes excitingly clear from this line of five—Voltaire, Feuerbach, Kierkegaard, [Christof 1860–1944] Schrempf, Dostoevsky, that the intellectual [*geistig*] battle is already a problem in itself, that having to fight for the intellectual [*geistig*] human being is not self-evident, and that [it] can become the human's destiny to what extent his fight consumes him and whether time and strength still remain to him to order and manage what he has fought for. This series opens with a selection from *Voltaire*—writings, letters, anecdotes, reports, opinions. Paul Sakman, his best living expert in Germany, the author of the magnificent Voltaire book [*Voltaire: Seine Geistesart und Gedanken,* Stuttgart: 1910], introduces him with a precious, furious, and oh-how-justified call to war against the "religious wave" of our days, out of which yet up to now no "goddess, no man, and no work" has emerged. How true! Or should it in the end have become apparent—perhaps really already at the end of the group started here by Sakman himself—that even more true is the old truth that you do not sense the devil just when he has already collared you? I mean, of course, a devil in the sense of Sakman and Voltaire, that is to say, a "religious" one.

Upon Voltaire's battle for the enlightened spirit against the "Infâme" there follows, introduced and accompanied by Ehrenberg himself, *Ludwig Feuerbach's* battle against "Infâme" *and* spirit, against Christianity and philosophy together. This "Philosophy of the Future" of 1840 will be for the majority today the greatest surprise of this series. For the notorious materialist reveals himself here as a thinker of outright alarming modernity, of a modernity that for the majority of those who practice philosophy today—is still in the future. For his battle against the philosophizing reason, which he equates with Christianity—and how right he is compared to the dephilosophized and dehumanized Christianity of his and partly even of our days—, does not fight, as it were, for the paper money, which is still worth a lot today, from the mint of the irrational that prints one doesn't know where, but for common sense, the real understanding of the real human being. It would be a pure joy to see how here the transcending *and* the "transcendental" night spirits cover the battlefield, if only after the fight the victor—and Feuerbach is victor—would still have had time to await the rising of the sun above the nightly battlefield. But that is a fighter's lot.

It is also the lot of *Kierkegaard* and of his German apostle *Christoph Schrempf* [1860], both of whom dominate the next two issues. From Kierkegaard, Schrempf offers a selection of biographical documents that do not recall the battle against Christianity that in his opinion is over, but rather the unfinished—and precisely for this reason still actual—battle for his [Kierkegaard's] own truth, as whose heir Schrempf rightly knows himself today—Schrempf, who also started as a fighter against the church and became a fighter with his own heresy. Schrempf publishes some of his own writings— an older, very clever, and very interesting writing on the theory of the battle of the spirit, which precisely in this framework once again becomes entirely alive—but what belongs even more to the topic of the group is what he has to say biographically when he edits and introduces himself. For the life that he describes here solves the question for the reader who till now has known only the writings (most worthy of reading) of this German thinker of the generation right after Nietzsche, why in all these writings the goal always emerges only as if on the horizon, and why therefore we deny to the thinker the final credibility that the fighter in him everywhere enforces; for this credibility is given only to him for whom the goal of his fight has already become the starting point of the life of a thinker. And to how few is this granted!

Only to the last one of the series. But to him only because the fight disappeared in his life and *only* that which was new, which was fought *for,* remained and became fruitful. *Dostoyevsky,* the poet of the future, even with his apparently polemical—anti-West, anti-German, antirevolutionary— remarks, which are contained in the selection, does not belong to the fighters. Later on, he did not like to read aloud from the biographical document of his development, the Siberian prison history—the introduction mentions it—"because it could be understood as an accusation"! If Ehrenberg, who publishes him himself with an introduction that, from the knowledge of decades, is pointed against yesterday's literary fashion, places him at the end of the group, then by this he may well have wanted to impress upon the reader that every fight gets its meaning and its right from that which lies beyond the fight.

Only from there does the fight get its right—not the fighter. And this is just what this series teaches: the greatness of the fighter, which remains great, even when his destiny spares him the greater and heavier responsibility of the victor.

6

A Pronouncement for a
Celebration of Mendelssohn

It would not be in keeping with the cruel gravity of this time nor with the modesty of the great man whom we are celebrating if we allow ourselves to be captivated by thoughtless delight in a festival. Already the month of the Jewish year demands introspection; so does the event of the Jewish present—we hope: not of Jewish history—may this day too demand contemplation!

Mendelssohn, the first German Jew in the difficult sense that accounts for both words in which we German Jews take our German Jewishness, has not been able to bequeath to us the protection under which he himself effected the new combination. That which has happened to him posthumously, in the heirs of his blood and of his name, out of

"Vorspruch zu einer Mendelssohnfeier" was written in the fall of 1929, and published in *Der Morgen* 5. Jahrgang, 4. Heft, 1929. Republished in *Kleinere Schriften,* 1937, and in *Zweistromland,* 1984, page 457.

whose brilliant rank, still blooming today in proud names, not a single one belongs to our community, this is the symbol of the menace into which he led the existence of our, his, spiritual descendants. Of a beloved menace, of one that we do not like to do without—not merely for the sake of the two beloved linked ones, of Judaism and of Germanness, but also out of love precisely for the danger, and in the belief that the fighting through and the living through of this danger are given to us as a task. But Mendelssohn led us defenseless into this danger, for his own protection was the worldview of his century, of whose first germs of disease—a magnificent sign for the authenticity of his philosophizing—he died. Thus, already the nineteenth century had to help itself along on its own, that is to say, un-Mendelssohnian way, and we, children of a time that has again changed, must again venture upon new paths.

Hear, therefore, as the opening note of our celebration in such seriousness and in such a—the Mendelssohnian!—way of thinking, the deeply moving words from his most personal work, the translation of the Psalms, which are now brought to you in a contemporary composition.

7

Lessing's Nathan

1

When I recently—M. Goldmann—Nathan not a Jew.—
Shylock he considered valid.

But immediately the first two scenes: "Poor child! What
are we humans?" The intonation in "But if only one human
being had," the sudden turn to deadly seriousness to down-
right sharpness in "Pride! and nothing but pride!," the in-
tensification of the tempo in "and what harm is it—" and
the final pathos in "is nonsense or blasphemy." But not to
harp on this, Nathan himself means it differently, after all.
He—in the scene with the Knight Templar—"knows that
all lands," "with a difference—yes—here also—With this
difference—." "How if I did not hate this people —." And

"Lessings Nathan," written in December 1919, was published
for the first time in *Zweistromland,* pages 449–53. It comprises
notes for a double lecture in Cassel. Gottfried Ephraim Lessing
(1729–81) wrote *Nathan der Weise* [Nathan the wise] in 1779.
Several English translations are available.

now Nathan's great reply: "Despise my people—. Are Christian and Jew sooner Christian and Jew than human being?"

But if we look here again *behind* Nathan, the sympathy that befalls him right away, does it really serve only as the bloodless specter of the human being? And is the turning point of the scene when the stony heart of the Knight Templar is melted, this sudden outbreak of—it's alright for us to say it—sentimentality not Jewish, of a sentimentality that immediately tries to hide itself modestly again from itself.

Here a general humanity is presupposed. It is the scene in which, with the exception of the concluding scene, perhaps in the purest way the trivial Nathan . . .

But how empty is this presupposition of the one humanity, as long as human beings are not willing. Here (as in the whole course of the play) it is the highest: that human beings recognize that they are of one family [*Geschlecht*]. But—then how, if one presupposed this? Human beings know it, of course, and in spite of it hate one another. Precisely brothers hate each other the most intensely perhaps— A poet of our day has fashioned this, indeed, he has composed the exact counterpart to the Knight Templar-Nathan scene: Beer Hofmann.

Lessing. Nathan's question "Are Christian and Jew sooner Christian and Jew than human being?" has its right, its entire right, as it is asked. Are we our people (mention that the word *people* here is not meant politically)? No, surely: the human being "is" not his people. The human being is not Judaism, Christianity. This [is] the error of the Middle Ages. (The story of Scotus: the tolerance of the time is that of the

Strasbourg Portals.) That is why the Middle Ages had to collapse and the "purely human" enter. The institutions had to stop being brides of God. They had to become houses for the children of God, the human beings. The human being more than his house. But not the unhoused one. Not the "pure," that is, the naked human being, the one who is cut loose, the cut flower in the vase. Rather only the housed one.

And now you see what the moment in which we live must answer to Nathan's question: Christian and Jew are not sooner Christian and Jew than human being, but rather a Christian and a Jewish human being are more than a naked human being and a naked institution. The Jewish human being—he has (or he must have), himself the power of a fact. That is the greatness of Zionism, it has *recognized it*. But we must all *do* it, and we all can, as easily or with as much difficulty as the Zionists. Today we can no longer *want* to remain naked human beings. We look "backward" but not in such a way that we would sacrifice our living life again to the life-destroying image of a holy institution. No, the institution may only be the house for us, we must know it and make it come true that we are more than the institution, living Jewish human beings.

And that is now the new solution to the problem of tolerance: "Only because you are Edom may I be Yaakov." No more the coexistence of two statues, no longer the indifferent confusion that one tried earlier to read out of Nathan the Wise, no: organic coherence, organic beside- , against- , and with-one-another (only the particular case can teach which of these three) of Jewish and Christian human beings.

To build them up, to *make* human being, not to remember that we *are* human beings, but human beings, prophetic ones (Nobel!) and that is why it is imperative to preserve the houses of spiritual life, it is imperative for us to preserve our Judaism as such a house. And only for this reason.

But for this reason in reality. And now—and I hope everything will now have become clearer to you through the world historical survey—look at Nathan. Here is the naked human being, whose familiarity is celebrated. Not: "because you are Edom may I be Yaakov," rather: because we are all the same, therefore let us mutually concede to each other the harmless differences of dress, food, and drink. It is a great symbol for this shallowness in the concluding scene where the archetypal difference of man and woman is denied in favor of the cool, fish-blooded brotherliness and sisterliness. The flatness of the family scene of the conclusion: uncle at best.

—But Nathan himself—he again gives the lie to himself: He is more than such an abstract human being. Act IV. A *Jewish* destiny. And we stand in Act IV. That best humanity is not ours.

And now let me finally lead you to the scene that you probably expected at the beginning. In the ring scene the Boccaccio-like turn: "for are not all of them founded in history." He himself knows it, too. He himself knows that the truth is only truth as an ancient coin that is weighted, as received and given as a gift, not as won, robbed; as created not as made. But then the upswing, the Sultan being swept along. From mere dumbness to humility. "God! God!" up to the closing word.

Even if Nathan does not see the spiritual order, that "only because you are Edom—," let him misunderstand it—the coexistence in it again genuine enlightenment—only for the sake of the tyranny of the one ring, but the main thing, that the test lies before us, that still—now just the last word.

ll

The Paul-story with Nathan.

[Wilhelm] Dilthey [1833–1911] on Lessing 1860: "What could a man be for us today who—."[1] As such he came out of the "agitated moral and int. [sic] circumstances" [Friedrich] Nietzsche [1844–1900].

Only for the Jews it remained Lessing. Only before a Jewish public would I like to speak about him.

Tragedy of the Jew until today: [Moses] Mendelssohn [1729–86] and Lessing.

That is they found themselves on the basis of the common abstraction of their positive religions.

And Lessing himself with this held before Mendelssohn, true, by giving his utmost, his own real essence which did not stand at the end of the days, but rather in the year 1789.

The friendship of Mendelssohn and Lessing was too messianic. It lacked the blood of the present time. Must this be? In any case: hence this basis does not endure. Today it is still occupied by us, no longer by the best Christians, no longer by the—Lessings. Thus they must be renewed.

And that is the only reason why I turn to Nathan, that is to say, only critically. (The aesthetic evaluation is a different aspect. We consciously leave it aside this evening. Perhaps another time.) And let our critique be led by the question: How far apart does a rift extend between Lessing's conscious tendency and his unconscious presentation? But in this connection first the question of intention, thus the prehistory.

And indeed we have united here, as in every proper story, two streams of stories, here the one of Lessing and the one of—Nathan. First, the one of Lessing. The remainders of the theology of the Enlightenment. Theology still in the eighteenth-century Protestant principle of Scripture. Lessing's attitude. The letter to his brother. Gymnastic. [Hermann Samuel] Reimarus [1694–1768].[2] Anti-idol. The Testament of John. His own researches. His own teachings. Nathan a stage. An aesthetic taking of breath. But how then—Nathan?! Did it have to be just in the Nathan? How does that happen?

Jews and Christians from Romans 11 and Isaiah 53 on. Kuzari [philosophical work by Jehuda Halevi (ca. 1080–1140)]. Rambam [Maimonides (1135–1204)]. [John] Duns Scotus [ca. 1266–1308]. Not the persecutions, rather that one endured them at all is the remarkable thing. Nicholas of Cusa [c.1400–1464]. In him already a new wave, for in the place of organic belonging together he puts tolerance. Boccaccio [1313–75]. The subterraneity of tolerant thought still in the age of the Reformation.

The breaking forth in the eighteenth century in connection with Leibniz, world expansion, classicism, England, Deists—Jews. The Encyclopedia[3] does not refer to them. But Lessing's "Jews" (In the margins:) In the Middle Ages the Jews were tolerated more, in modern times less than the others, that is a characteristic feature for the change of the concept of tolerance.

Mendelssohn, the man of our destiny. The fact *that* he is a Jew. —But of interest Mendelssohn's covering up of this fact. Then came [Johann Caspar] Lavater [1741–1801].

Tell of the Lavater controversy: the emergence of the Jewish consciousness in Mendelssohn. But what a consciousness! More messianically colored than the time allowed (Proof: the Mendelssohn family [i.e., all were baptized]) and yet as messianic as the time demanded. For certainly it saved the messianic Jew. Thus, wedged in between the demand of the time (in the highest sense) and the necessity to preserve ourselves, are we today. Zionism is attempting a way out. In this everything is good except this one thing, that it is a way out. Out of serious problems there is no way out, only a through. But Mendelssohn stands at the beginning of an epoch, for him there is not yet a problem.

Thus the elements for Nathan are all there. From Lessing's side as from the side of his material. What happens now.

Apportionment of light and shadows. Nathan as Jew. The turning point of the history of the ring. Surmounting of the mere thoughts of tolerance, above all of the indifference through the bloody demand of the "thousand thousand years." The messianic prospect of the end. No children. Refuted actually already through the story of the prayer of the fourth act (which one only needs to examine in order to look beyond the ridiculous fight about Lessing's "Determinism"). "From myself to myself." "Misunderstanding." We stand in act 4, not in act 5, the one that has not turned out anemic by chance. To forget that, to forget it again and again is our Jewish right. To remind of it, to remind of it again and again is a Jewish duty. Do not let us forget the word that I want to give you today as the last one to take along with you, so that you remember it: "The thousand thousand years are not yet over." "Ancient coin that is weighed"! You yourselves be the Sultan.

8

On Lessing's Style of Thinking

Among the great men of the German classic, Lessing is the least understood. He was such a thoroughly *oral* human being that, in order to understand his true meaning, one has to keep in mind in every utterance at any given time its place in the actual conversation to which it belonged for Lessing himself. Only from this can he know if Lessing meant it with an exclamation mark or a question mark or even with a dash. It is very seldom a period, for the period is the death of the conversation.

Thus, he himself intended many of his most famous lunges only as feints, and only because the world-historical parade was already wretchedly weak, they penetrated them and thus—contrary to the actual intention of the brilliant fencer therefore—became "bloody ones."

"Zu Lessings Denkstil" appeared in the *Lessing-Nummer C. V.-Zeitung* of 18 Jan. 1929. Reprinted in *Kleinere Schriften,* 1937 and *Zweistromland,* 1984, page 455.

9

Stefan George

Dear Mr. Haas,

You put me in an awkward position.[1] I got to know George too late for him to play a role in my development. At that time in 1907 I already moved, even if blindly, toward the pole of the intellectual field of force that lies precisely opposite that other pole around which George circles. True, someone who does not believe as I do in the inseparability of intellect [*Geist*] and speech [*Sprache*] could expect linguistic influences in spite of the intellectual foreignness. But when I think about the contemporary speakers who have shaped my speech—of the earlier ones, as probably for the whole generation of those who are in their forties today, Hölderlin and the late Goethe—I find: around 1905 Spit-

Answer to an inquiry concerning Stefan George and German intellectual life by *Literarische Welt*. It was published in the issue of 13 July 1928, and reprinted in *Kleinere Schriften,* 1937 and in *Franz Rosenzweig: De Mensch und Sein Werk. Briefe und Tagebücher,* 2. Band, *1918–1929,* Letter 1204 (The Hague: Martinus Nijhoff, 1979), p. 1191.

teler, around 1910 Rilke, around 1911 C. Philips, since 1913 Eugen Rosenstock, around 1918 Werfel, since 1922 in our collaboration Buber, and most recently perhaps Ludwig Strauß.

10

The Concert Hall on the Phonograph Record

Introduction

Radio and phonograph records together have in our times, expanded the accessibility of the concert hall to an unforeseen extent as regards space and time. With this they have carried a historical development to its point of maturity, whose beginnings still go back barely 150 years. For the accessibility of the concert hall—like that of the museum and the gallery—starts in cautious beginnings not until the

Written from spring 1928 to fall 1929 as reviews of selected phonograph records. Appeared in the *Feuilleton* of the *Kasseler Tageblatt* in the numbers from 13 May, 3 June, 18 July, 4 Sept., 30 Oct. 1928, 27 Jan., 7 Apr., 19 July, and 23 Nov. 1929. Reprinted as "Der Konzertsaal auf der Schallplatte" in *Kleinere Schriften*, 1937, and in *Zweistromland: Kleinere Schriften zu Glauben und Denken*, ed. Reinhold and Annemarie Mayer (Dordrecht: Martinus Nijhoff, 1984), pages 427–48.

decades immediately before the French Revolution and only generally prevails in the decades that follow it. It is truly an achievement of the nineteenth, of the bourgeois century. Out of the festival hall of the castle, the chamber of the country seat, the arts step out into premises that are basically accessible to everyone and actually—this too is characteristic of the bourgeois-democratic century—at least to the solvent educated class.

This is a development that does not remain limited to the political and social side; not merely the public, art itself is influenced by it. The Beethoven symphony, for instance, would, by its essence, have demanded those great public halls for itself, which the epoch built for it. "Be embraced, millions!" [from the Ninth Symphony] cannot be sung into a closed circle. The physically present public is no longer a circle, no longer a community, but rather a representative of humanity—it is this precisely in its colorful and haphazard combination. Its spatial expansion to the hundreds of thousands who share in the listening to the radio, its temporal expansion to the future listeners of the phonograph record that was recorded at the performance—this expansion is only the legitimate conclusion of the development that arose with the building of the first public concert halls and with the creation of the first works that were suitable only for them.

In the following we are going to discuss the major works of the classical and modern concert hall, as far as they exist on the phonograph record and have become known to me. - - -

Chamber Music

With the entrance of music into the public sphere, there is historically connected the separation of an art that remains intimate: chamber music. The Bachian [Johann Sebastian Bach (1685–1750)] orchestra was still what is today called chamber orchestra. At the same moment when there emerges with the modern symphony the art form that in its further development was to create the concert hall for itself, there emerges in the string quartet the central type of a domestic music that is just as specific. True, it is also drawn into the expansion of the public type of concert [*Konzertwesen*]; indeed, starting from the last quartets of [Ludwig van] Beethoven [1770–1827] a considerable part of the literature lies beyond the capacity of normal dilettantes. But their actual homeland will never be the concert hall; it opens itself entirely only to him who, playing himself, fights for it in ceaseless effort or to him who can present it today in ever renewed listening, independent of his ability to play, between his own four walls.

There is one of the six quartets by [Joseph] Haydn [1732–1809] that are already dedicated to [Wolfgang Amadeus] Mozart [1756–91], the one in G Major, op. 76, no. 1, flawlessly played by the Budapest Quartet. Let him who has registered under the art historical *fable convenue* [appropriate fable] of "Papa Haydn," the only pioneer of the "new music" of 1750, though not its inaugurator, who became and remained uniquely classical, let him hear the broad, "Beethovian" song of this adagio, the perfectly scherzolike min-

uet that bursts open the dance form, this finale which overflows with ideas of genius.

The Amar Quartet plays Mozart's E-flat Major Quartet
out of the six that were dedicated to Haydn. It is notewor-
thy for an ear that comes from the nineteenth century, how
objectively, how completely avoiding all that has to do with
feeling, this most modern of the present quartet group plays
Mozart! At the same time, though, convincingly; for surely
there is in the Mozart with whom we grew up a piece of
that which today is called "romantic," when one looks at
the whole of the nineteenth century, and in this Mozart the
formal, more precisely, the rhythmical element, was not suf-
ficiently emphasized; just this is brought out by the Amar
Quartet, in which the great rhythmist Paul Hindemith sits
at the viola desk.

Beside Beethoven's well-known youthful work—of course
better known in the piano arrangements for four hands than
in the precious timbre of the original—beside the much
loved and charming septet, played by a Berlin group, we
will mention not less than four string quartets by Beethoven. From opus 18, the sixth one, in B Major, with the
program music of the final movement (wrongly designated
on the records as two movements), in which, against a painful "Malinconia"—a very un-Dürer-like Melancholy—a
round-dance developing in a clockworklike way storms
along in ever new repetitions and yet prevails only after it
has revealed the seriousness hidden inside it. By the mature
master the C Major Quartet, op. 59, no. 3, with the concluding fugue and that andante—presaging harmonies and

moods that are Brahms-like, even Reger-like—of that [Max] Reger [1873–1916], who looks back to [Johannes] Brahms [1833–97]. A transition then is made to the later Beethoven, played by the Amar Quartet, the F Minor quartet, whose opus number 95 designates only the time of its appearance, but which in spite of that prepares the "late quartets" in the conciseness, boldness, and reckless divergence of its language. Of those there is the E-flat Major Quartet, op. 127, played (as also the Quartets in B Major and C Major) by a quartet in which one hears the bliss with which it plunges into the sea of inconceivable beauty. If only a company would decide also to produce the four younger siblings of this work, opp. 130, 131, 132, 135; it is the noblest and ultimately also the most gratifying task in the entire field of phonograph records of chamber music.

For the [Franz] Schubert [1797–1828] year the company that was most eager for a serious musical repertory will produce a whole series of Schubert's works. In the meantime the earliest of the string quartets has appeared, the northern-balladlike one in A Minor, op. 29, played by the Deman Quartet, and the famous piano quintet in A Major, op. 114, with the variations on the song of the trout, this great musical idealization of Viennese essence, played by the Gewandhaus quartet players with van Pauer on the grand piano and Findeisen on the bass. The posthumous first movement of a C Minor quartet should not be forgotten either, which would deserve a fame similar to that of the Unfinished Symphony. — By Schubert there is here still the powerful piano trio in B-flat Major, op. 99; how here the cello of the great living master of the instrument, Casals, harmonizes with the violin and the piano of his trio colleagues, Thibaud and [Alfred] Cortot [1877–1962], that must convert anybody who is still skeptical about the phonograph record.

From the romantic century there is only one work, but a monumental one: the only piano quintet by Brahms, which roars forth autumnally, by the great master who today has fallen out of favor with the spirit of the times, played by Harold Bauer and the Flonzaley Quartet, which originally emerged as a house quartet of a Maecenas. The harmonic fullness of this music, which cannot be surpassed, can illuminate why one could not proceed on this path any further and why—already with the late Brahms himself and then with Reger—it had to come to that loosening and lightening of the harmony which had become all too dense, which was going to lead to the "linear" style of the New Music. Reger's String Trio in A Minor, op. 77b, one of his most immediately accessible works, truly shows so rightly this paternal relationship of Reger to the New Music—but then of course it was played by Caspar and the Brothers Hindemith!

Of the living ones, the chamber music phonograph records (besides the Quintet for Winds, op. 23 in A-sharp Major, which is of course not actually significant, or very attractive, composed by the Hungarian Lendvai, who now resides in Germany, and performed by the Gewandhaus winds) carries only the first two of the four movements of Hindemith's—so far unfortunately sole—(for the time being?) String Trio, op. 34. The work is again played by Caspar and the Hindemiths, and thus is an authentic rendering. The first movement, marked "Toccata" in spite of the string instruments, is framed and supported by a sturdy theme sounded in unison, a wild alternating concertizing of three instruments. The second movement—"slow and with great tranquillity"—weaves an infinitely tender web of voices, which unfolds more and more entrancingly with each hearing—that is, as soon as the ear is ready to listen to the voices not as one, as we were accustomed to do, but to listen to them apart: that is to say, basically to listen in the way that pre-Haydn music demands—and as in any case we lay people have become unaccustomed to in the nineteenth century, even for Bach.

It is one of the marks of this return of the present day to the pre-Haydn epoch, that that separation of chamber music and symphony, with which the new age started around 1750, begins to lose its meaning for the present day: today we write, without perceiving the name as an inner contradiction—"chamber symphonies."

Beethoven's Piano Sonatas

As everyone knows, the microphone is unyielding precisely with respect to the sound of the piano. A radio transmission of pure piano music most of the time has something hard, clacking. Strangely enough, the matter is more favorable with the phonograph record. For instance, in the piano part of the Schubert Trio already discussed or in the little records with "Ecossaise" and "Bagatelle" by Beethoven, one is hardly aware of any difference from the authentic sound of the piano, and when Lamond plays the first movement of the *Moonlight Sonata,* a most exacting piece, just because it is so easy that every dilettante "can also do it"—one hears every fine detail of his famous, soft, "singing" touch.

But even if it were not entirely so—and since there are many more people who hear the grass growing than those who frankly admit that they are not capable of doing so, many will always explain that they "cannot get over the mechanical"—even if it were not entirely so: it doesn't really matter that much! This is the place for a general remark: In all the arts we all tend toward a snobbish over-evaluation [*sic*] of the reproductions [*Wiedergabe*] as compared to the art work itself. People who hardly have any idea how an etching is made would nevertheless—assuming that they had been told which is the original and which is the reproduction—sooner bite off their tongues than admit that the page from the national printer's is just as beautiful as or even (perhaps as compared to a "late state" of the original) more beautiful than the "authentic" Rembrandt out of the engraving cabinet. In truth, as long as there is a certain, not too low, minimum quality of the reproduction, so if, for instance, in the case of the etching there is no autotyping and in the case of phonograph records we have no gramophone horn recording, the work alone is the deciding factor. The same applies to reproducing artists; here, too, the work alone is important, once certain minimum demands have been fulfilled. Beethoven remains Beethoven, even when the concertmaster of the local orchestra is playing the violin, and kitsch remains kitsch, even when [Fritz] Kreisler [1878–1962] plays it.

To come back to the sonatas: before me are the *Pathétique* and the *Moonlight Sonata,* played by the Beethoven interpreter, who, next to d'Albert, has determined the image of Beethoven for my generation, Frederick Lamond, and the *Pathétique,* the *Moonlight Sonata* and the *Waldstein Sonata,* played by the successor to van Pauer as director of the Stuttgart Conservatory, Wilhelm Kempff. So, the young master in his early thirties [plays] beside the old master already in his sixties, the younger one doing more building, the older doing more singing, the former working out the contrasts more, the latter drawing everything more into the unity of the whole—one should notice how with Kempff, for instance, the figuration as such stands out in relation to the melody and how his runs "are like strings of pearls," whereas in the case of Lamond, for whom they also sing into the *Melos,* they "flow." Granted all difference of individuality, still the difference in how the different generations see Beethoven is probably also operative, the image of the "composing" Beethoven, with whom we grew up, and that of the forming one, who has to be, as it were, taken in with the feeling of space, whom the youngest ones seek.

Sacred and Spiritual Choral Music

It is characteristic for the essence of all renaissances that the founders of the opera in the sixteenth century, just like their reformers in the three following centuries, always believed that they were creating "ancient tragedies" for the present—without any idea that Christian Europe had already for a long time produced an art of its own that was at least of equal rank to the Attic tragedies, and that it passed on from generation to generation in living cultivation: the musical mass and all the forms of liturgical music that blossomed alongside it. That which they longingly sought to retrieve, they already had, without knowing it, in accustomed and familiar possession. It is not merely the fact that in the mass a genuine descendant of antique tragedy towers into our centuries, a descendent that is still immediately visual in the Eastern Church with the bearded Christ-mask of its priest, with the painting depicting columns and metopes and of the three portals of their "panels,"—yes even the function of these three portals and the name of the center one, King's Entrance—and finally, with its postponement of the decisive event, of the metamorphosis itself, into the inner room that is separated by the panel, into which the parishioners can only look through the open "King's Entrance." Rather this observation of historical development is less important than the fact that, here as there, art adapts itself as a servant in the worship and the fact that yet, on the other hand, just for this reason, here as there, an exoneration of art is reached from the baser interests of the common material tension, such as the free work of art always strives for and never attains.

I have here individual pieces of liturgical choral music and smaller samples of great works: from the sixteenth century two widely arching choruses filling a single melodic breath from Palestrina's [1525–94] *Pope Marcillus Mass,* the "Sanctus" and the "Benedictus," both sung by the Berlin Cathedral Choir under Rüdel; and, sung by the silvery Italian voices of the Casimir Choir, choruses of the two old "Vene-

tians" Marenzio and Viadana, the former full of stimulating
freshness, the latter, the beginning of Psalm 33, a most tender rejoicing; finally—the Basilica Choir, the Choir of the
Hedwig Church in Berlin—by the great maestro of the
north, Lasso, a composition, radiant in glasslike eight voices,
of the verses of Psalm 89. From the seventeenth century,
two works of Protestant music: by [Heinrich] Schütz [1585–
1672], the great pre-Bach German musician, whose boy-
hood education and first activity as a man by the way took
place in Kassel, the bewitchingly bittersweet final movement
of his German mass, sung by the Berlin Cathedral Choir;
unfortunately the only piece by him available on record,
and, sung by the Basilica Choir, is an immediately appealing
composition for six voices, of the conclusion of the Lu-
theran Twenty-fourth Psalm by Schütz's successor [Andreas]
Hammerschmidt [1611 (or 1612)–75]. From the eighteenth
century, works are available in which even we laymen detect
the connection with the "secular" music of the century, a
connection that is yet always present, at least in the case of
living, not artificial sacred music—for genuine love of God
cannot be expressed differently from genuine earthly love—
which we however do not perceive for the earlier times,
because from those times we consciously possess only sacred
art, which is the only one that benefits from the conserving
power of the worship: two choral works (for which what
has just been said naturally does not apply on account
of their older origin) and two fugues by Bach, sung by
Straube's St. Thomas Church Singers, the choir that com-
bines the proudest tradition with a splendidly youthful modernity; an already rococolike happy Marian hymn of the

Viennese Welsh Caldara, sung by the Cathedral Choir; the lamenting loveliness of the first movement of the *Stabat Mater* of [Giovanni Batista] Pergolesi [1710–36], modernized by Irmler from the original, pure duet form by a partial transcription in choral voices, whose choir sings it; finally, a piece from parts of Mozart's *Requiem,* completed with congenial genius by [Franz Xavier] Süßmayr [1766–1803], sung by the London Philharmonic Choir. From the nineteenth century, women's choirs (Irmler) by [Franz] Schubert, among them a German Twenty-third Psalm; and by the Temple-Church Choir, in English, of course, compositions of [Felix] Mendelssohn [1809–47] for voice, among them an extensive composition on the Fifty-fifth Psalm. If here, stronger in Mendelssohn, weaker in Schubert, the secularization of the century is noticeable in a certain smooth excess of beauty, then the comforting certainty from the powerful stride of the great opening movement of [Anton] Bruckner's [1824–96] *Te Deum* (to which a fragment of the second-to-last movement—in itself very beautiful—is surprisingly added) brings the comforting certainty that "centuries" have no power over the relationship of the human being to God—because it not only depends on the human being, but also on God.

There are more substantial samples of several major works of sacred music.

From Bach's *B Minor Mass* the two tremendous songs of praise of the angels from the Old and New Testaments, the "Sanctus," where the voices float and call to each other, and the "Gloria," which comes shooting down on trumpet beams, both sung by the Royal Choral Society in a public performance on 24 April 1926.

From the *St. Matthew Passion* the first choir with its three choruses, not, as usual (even with Ochs himself earlier on) in a powerfully graphic diffusion of contrasts, but dashed through by Ochs with his Philharmonic Choir with an extreme Expressionistic dramatic effect; one needs to hear it more often to find once more the familiar piece in this intensifying translation from [Albrecht] Dürer's [1471–1528] world into [Matthias] Grünwald's [ca. 1460/70–1528]. The concluding choir we have twice: by the Westminster Abbey Chor and by the Berlin Kittelchor. The German recording [was played] in the tempo of a funeral march, heavily armored as we are accustomed to, the English one strangely hurried for our taste. Out of the action itself the dramatically deeply moving outburst of the "ideal spectator"— Schiller's definition of the antique chorus—after the capture (Kittelchor with Lotte Leonard and Emmi Leisner) and two of the chorales, in which once, before the era of the concert performances, the entire community transformed itself into those "ideal spectators."

[George Frideric] Händel's [1685–1759] *Messiah* is available in two great selections of his choruses, six choruses from a performance of the Royal Choral Society conducted by Sargent on 2 April 1926, and the Overture and seven choruses, of which five are identical with the older recording, conducted by Beecham. What Händel is can actually only be fully felt when unbounded openness of his music to earth and heaven is fitted to the terse speed of the original English—a pleasure in itself, even if just here in the splendid compilation of the *Messiah* text, which goes back to Händel himself, the usual German translations were not so despicably bad.

The two English recordings barely differ in conception, apart from differences of tempo. If this already indicates a national tradition, then it becomes a certainty through a possible comparison with two German recordings for the most famous chorus of all, the "Hallelujah": The Kittelchor well represents the German tradition of performance: a booming force that scarcely allows details to emerge from the mighty overall impression. The Irmlerchor sings it already in a more transparent and organized manner. But still, what a great distance [there is] even from this interpretation to the charming articulation (reminiscent of the early-rococo style) of the splendor of the two English performances, which in the overall impression, yet sweep along, that is to say, sweep along in rococo style! Note, for instance, the moving pianissimo entering of the choral recollection in the words that in the German text read: "Der Herr wird König sein" [The Lord will be king] or the flashing lightning of the small fanfare before the second one, "Herr der Herrn" [Lord of Lords], neither of which can be noticed at all in the German performances. Obviously the land of tradition [England] here, as in so many other regions, has kept a piece of the eighteenth century that in our case is smothered under the massiveness of the nineteenth.

From the most beautiful post-Händel oratorio, Haydn's *Creation,* the Basilica Choir sings the end of the third day of Creation, the Händel-like fugal choir "Stimmt an die Saiten" [Start the strings], and the concluding chorus of the first part about the Nineteenth Psalm, steeped in color, with the enchanted archangel solo voices woven into the choir.

What I just mentioned—a weaving of solo voices into the choir—is more than a technical advance. Maybe it was originally applied to the "dramatization," as it stems from the opera, especially from operatic finales: why since the end of the eighteenth century it spread so quickly over the sacred choir literature has deeper reasons. The "we" of the praying community supports itself by the hundredfold "I" of its limbs, yet they can only say "I" because the "we" of the community carries it. This most intimate reciprocal interweaving of me and everyone now finds its form of expression. And with this the greatest work of the whole genre has become possible, which in Bach's *B Minor Mass* still did not rise above the magnificent objectivity of a graphic juxtaposition of the choirs and the solo pieces: Beethoven's *Missa Solemnis*.

It has recently been available from the first to last note in a splendid performance and technically in the most perfect recording imaginable [featuring:] Kittelchor, the Philharmonic Orchestra, the Solo Quartet: Lotte Leonard and Emmy Land; Eleanor Schloßhauer-Reynolds; A. M. Topitz and E. Transley; W. Guttmann and H. Schey; Solo violin: W. Hanke. These eleven records, in themselves already remarkable as the most extensive uninterrupted work on the phonograph record, are a proper claim to glory for the firm—and for the one who owns it, a delightful possession.

People, including myself, have tried to interpret many a conspicuous individual trait of the *Missa Solemnis,* such as, for instance, the gigantic weight of the word *Credo* that overshadows the object of faith, the unending elaboration of the "Leben der kommenden Welt" [Life of the world to come] in contrast to the briefly treated raising of the dead, the most realistic, wholly this-worldly pacifist treatment of the concluding plea for peace, as if here Beethoven's modern piety were destroying the old cultic form. I do not know whether today I would still repeat that. After all, Beethoven also originally undertook the writing of this mass for a quite definite church occasion, and in the this-worldly conception of the plea for peace, Haydn had already preceded him at the beginning of that quarter of a century of international wars. I suppose we're dealing here (just as in Bach's great *Mass,* of which he, as we know, performed only individual parts in the public worship) rather with external reasons of size, which closed the church gates against the work and drove it into the concert hall. In itself it would exercise the strongest effect precisely there, through the interweaving of the solo voices—an effect that would be as unique for us, who are accustomed to the concert halls, as the effect of *Antigone* on the Athenian audience with the effect of the book or even of a performance. For the art work as such is performed with perfection; but I believe a kitchen maid who had to wash up in the Ottheinrichsbau [the Ottheinrich building] of the Heidelberg Castle was influenced by the building—including the façade!—more profoundly in its entire essence, in every word and every movement, than the most finely cultured traveler who admires the remaining façade from the courtyard today.

The—luckily only partial—destruction of the genuine intrinsic value of sacred music is not indicative of the turning point that also occurred in this region in 1800, but rather of something positive: the new emergence of a music of the spirit—of the spiritual beside the sacred song.

It is not a matter of contrasting something worldly with something sacred. That had also existed earlier. Worldly and sacred song, worldly and sacred music move side by side. The new element is that alongside the sacred music and competing with it there emerges one that flies over the world just as much and then, of course, does not overcome the world, but rather transforms the world, which demands the concert hall as a space for its ringing out, just because it is a neutral space that is open to everyone. The prerequisite for the appearance of such a music is the unique encounter of a living philosophy with a living literature, as happened around 1800 in Germany, circumscribed in terms of persons by the names Fichte, Schiller, Goethe, Hegel; geographically through the names Jena and Weimar. It is impossible to imagine how things would have developed if Beethoven had been in Dresden (which would have been biographically fully possible), instead of being in Vienna, where the news of Schiller's death reached a full five weeks after the fact, and if then, possibly through Councillor Körner a living personal relationship to Thüringen would have started. As it was, the contact of the new spirit and the new music happened only across spatial distance; its first and unsurpassed monument is the last movement of the Ninth Symphony.

Two recordings are available. The one under Fried with the Kittelchor and the Orchestra of the State Opera, best model of a German performance, astonishing in terms of technical reproduction in the rendering of the multiplicity of the orchestral colors—the rumbling of the double-basses at the beginning!—and an English one under Coates, who after all spent his school years and first years of employment in Germany, with the London Philharmonic Choir and excellent soloists, especially beautiful the very bright, almost tenorlike baritone. The impression is deeply moving when one suddenly hears in English the words of the "immortal Schiller"—to echo Beethoven's original setting of the introductory bass recitativo: a wholly immediate experience of the one humanity; those who met the Bible for the first time in the garment of a new language must have had a similar experience.

The final benefit of the sacred song, the combined singing of the I and the We now becomes the cradle of the newborn song of the spirit. Only that there the basic form is that the voice frees itself from the choir—for instance, as in the first beats of the *Missa*—that here the basic form is that the voice summons and awakens the choir. There humanity before God, here man in humanity—and God only sensed, only sought, only "above the firmament."

Out of the whole rich literature of the cantatalike musical compositions of classical-romantic world-literature and literature of life the record offers only one work so far. We don't even have Brahms's compositions on Goethe's *Harzreise im Winter,* on Schiller's most beautiful poem *Die Nänie,* on [Friedrich] Hölderlin's *Hyperions Schicksalslied* [Song of destiny]. That one work is [Gustav] Mahler's setting to music of the five *Kindertotenlieder* by [Friedrich] Rückert, sung by Rehkemper, the baritone from Munich. It is in its whole attitude a solo cantata, not a song cycle, even in the orchestral treatment, though that is decidedly like chamber music. The moving effect, even more moving in the silent despair than in the outbursts, extorts from the anxious heart of the listener the question that certainly confronts the questionability of all art and that we, were we only always really deeply moved would have to ask always: the question whether suffering—may become beauty for us.

Orchestral Concertos

The orchestral concerto, as Mozart introduced it among the musical genres, is only loosely connected with what was formerly called concerto. Nevertheless, just in this genre more than in any other, elements of older music making have escaped into the nineteenth-century cultivation of music. The musician, as the artist altogether, learns in the nineteenth century, the century novel about the artist, to take himself solemnly seriously. The work becomes confession, by-product of the biography, whereas previously it had something of the modesty of craftsmanship. It gains a rarity value, precisely the value of the "life experience" ["*Erlebnis*"]: from Beethoven on and with Beethoven himself the numbers of the works of the older ones that sound strange to us today, like fairy tales, diminish; the musician now takes his pride no longer in composing because he can compose, but rather only in composing when he has to compose.

Thus the joyous, sportive element disappears from the music business, and only now most recently it enters again, in the entourage of the New Music. In the nineteenth century it had maintained a sanctuary only in the instrumental concerto. Only here had the virtuoso, at times, but certainly not always, remained the equal partner with the composer in a personal union: the composer writes here for the virtuoso, mostly for quite a specific virtuoso, and the destiny of the work is not, as usual, the diagonals of the forces of composer and public, but is essentially decided by the virtuoso, who "becomes part" of it. Also the improvisation, the essential distinctive mark of the art of virtuosity, which formerly in the times of the thoroughbass was simply a matter of course—at one time there was a specification of execution *come sta,* "as it stands"!—holds a place that was felt to be legitimate only in the cadenzas of the orchestral concerto; only here the virtuoso may still exercise his old seigneurial right of the first night in the century of scientific editions: to invent on the basis of what he finds; a right, which today seems to us so wrong, indeed nearly blasphemous, that even the contemporary report that Beethoven, at the first performance, had played his G Major concerto "very mischievously," that is (as by chance we can even prove here), with free flourishes, makes us shudder slightly, as if to say: "But is that allowed?"

The form of the more recent orchestral concerto is the result of the combination of this virtuoso element that escaped into it with the new musical principle of form, of the form that is filled with the flow of changing feelings. More precisely: from the reciprocal exchange between the solo and tutti, to the new sonata form of the symphony. At the same time the older component, the alternation of the voice of the orchestra and the orchestral chorus, is itself changed in accordance with the new century; to the mere charm of tone, at which this alternation aimed earlier, the attempt is now added to make full use of it dramatically up to the application of entirely programmed music (as for instance the concertizing viola in [Hector] Berlioz's [1803–69] *Harold Symphony* [*Harold in Italy*]).

In concluding this introductory remark, let us still stress, in order to rule out an obvious misunderstanding: it is not that for the artist of the old style, experience would have been meaningless, and for the artist of the new style, virtuosity would have been. One needs indeed only to think of Bach's profound fantasy, of Beethoven's thematic work, to see the whole absurdity of such a claim. But what is different is what the age expects from the artist, and accordingly, which aspect of his artistry the artist shows to the public and which he keeps privately for himself. So we are dealing here with a temporal-sociological, not an artistic-psychological difference.

Now to the records! Concertos in the older form: [George Frideric] Händel's [1685–1759] Organ Concerto no. 4 in F Major in Four Movements, played by Walter Fischer, rolling along in happy brightness; its first movement—unfortunately not the whole—we have once more, boomingly and at the same time delicately played by Maestro Sittard on the organ of St. Michaelis in Hamburg—one thinks one feels the tones flowing down from the vault. From Bach's piano concertos unfortunately only isolated movements, from the

"Italian," the first; from the F Minor Concerto the first and the second (incomprehensible that the company did not allow another record in order to complete both works of three movements!) played by Alice Ehlers on the harpsichord for whose austere, nonreverberating "pointed" tone this music is originally meant.

The new concerto form: Of Beethoven's five piano concertos, the profoundly happy G Major Concerto, op. 58, played by Karol Szreter with the two Rubinstein cadenzas, which overwhelm somewhat the atmosphere of this concerto with their virtuosity. Of major works of the romantics: Mendelssohn's Violin Concerto, which is still fresh and always will be, in the noble melancholy of the first movement, in the sweet tenderness of the second, in the elfin charm of the third, played by Kreisler's magic bow; and the first of [Frédéric] Chopin's two piano concertos, the one in E minor, with the fiery richness of its musical thoughts and the glittering splendor of its performance, played by Brailowsky. Finally, from the "new German" late-romantic period, [Franz] Liszt's [1811–86] two concertos, the one in E flat major, still divided into movements, played again by Brailowsky, and the one in A major which has all the sorcery of the new instrumentation, and which is written in the single movement of a "Symphonic Poem," played by Pembaur, the current avowed interpreter of Liszt.

In these "Symphonic Concertos" by Liszt the borders of the genre are actually expanded, and in particular with their apparent progress: the instrument in spite of all required virtuosity yet basically is no longer treated in a virtuoso manner, that is to say, no longer in its specific instrumental character; the style is not pianolike, but—I say it spite-fully—like a piano reduction, the piano has to appear now as a full partner of the orchestra, now as a singing human voice, now as any of the instrumental voices or groups of voices of the orchestra, but never as it were as—a piano. I confess that I, quite apart from the question of taste, in the tonal language of Liszt would place this handling of the pi-ano, although the ground has already been prepared for it here and there by the German Classicists, far below the treatment of the instrument, as for instance in that Chopin concerto, where no one can forget for a moment that one is hearing a piano, which basically behind all the mechanical improvements of the modern concert grand piano, brings out the original instrument of humanity, which lies within the piano: the harp, whose strings the minstrel touches.

Schubert

To the universal very unsentimental rule that every post-humous fame needs some fame, great or small, within the artist's lifetime, for it to come about, perhaps Hölderlin and Van Gogh are the exceptions proving the rule, but Schubert is not. If one considers that he died so young, he conquered the Viennese public already in his lifetime by the essential innovation that he offered: with his songs. The best men surrounded him as the center point of his circle of friends, Beethoven from his seclusion at least gave his blessing, a series of great singers enthused the public with his songs, right up to the emperor's court. A consolation for his friends at his early death was: "He departs the world at least with fame!" The only ones still missing were the publishers; at least: they were happy to publish, only not to pay; in this they are somewhat excused by Schubert's provocative helplessness in business matters.

And that the fame, apparently stubbornly, first latched only onto the songs, and left the instrumental works to posthumous fame, that is also a fate that is not spared even to the most successful ones. Goethe's lyrics of his old age, especially *Der westöstliche Diwan* [The west-eastern divan], did not win over an audience until our century; until shortly before the war there was no edition of *Pandora* by itself, and his most passionate iambic drama, *The Natural Daughter* is today still banned by the Weimar schoolmasters: as smooth as marble and as cold as marble. Success, even of successful people, has its whims. If indeed they are whims, and not rather the instinctive but healthy reaction of the appetite of the public against a food that in this historical moment is still indigestible for its stomach. A public that only now was occupied with accepting Beethoven, would, only with difficulty, have been able to comprehend Schubert at the same time. Construction and dismantling [*Aufbau und Abbau*] cannot happen at the same time. The elements that Beethoven had just compressed flow apart again in Schubert. From a historical perspective, he is, in his orchestral compositions, the turning point from the classic to the romantic of the century. No achievement has yet been lost of Beethoven's classical period (by Beethoven only the early and middle one is understood), but the result is yet finally quite a new one which really only could be understood at the height of the romantic development. Externally, Schubert did not abandon or burst open the formal cycle of the classical; but he shifts the domination of the dramatic form of the sonata movement to the lyrically indulging recapitulation of the variation movements. Not merely in the sense that variation movements gave to his works a name and popularity, but in the deeper sense, that in the sonata movement itself the thematic groups no longer have the reciprocal dramatic tension, but rather the new group appears when pleasure in the old has been exhausted; after a while the refreshed senses can dip again into the first group of themes: so, out of this rondo- and variationlike treatment of the sonata form, there arises what [Robert] Schumann [1810–56] called Schubert's "heavenly length"—he can never get enough of it, never listen enough to the melodies ringing out in him. And from the "heavenly length" there leads a straight path to the "endless melody," from which yet on the other hand Schubert, the classical one, is still far distanced, much farther than the late Beethoven who creates at the same time, but shrouded in the magic hat of the prophet.

The fact that Schubert, of course, even today did not yet really escape the fate of the whimsically choosing recording is indicated by the phonograph record literature. There is missing, to name only the greatest ones, the Octet, the G Major Quartet, the Quartet Movement in C Minor, the great piano works with the exception of the *Wanderer* Fantasy, and above all the String Quartet.

I have before me: the *Unfinished Symphony* in two recordings: played once by the Berlin Philharmonica under Prüwer, with which the company itself again overtakes its own recording under Blech, which is only a few months older; and once played by the Orchestra of the Berlin State Opera under Schillings, with a powerful—incidentally also technically powerful—working out of the thunderclouds in the sky of this most blessèd symphony. Also in two recordings the *Trout Quintet,* one played by the Gewandhaus Quartet and v. Pauer, the other under the direction of the self-assured violin of Edith Lorand and with Raucheisen at the piano, the two differing, to my mind, only in details, probably because in its magnificent clarity the work leaves hardly any room for different views. The Deman-Quartet plays the posthumous D Minor String Quartet, Schubert's "Media in vita," with a ravishing power, not interrupted for a moment, and the next best-known quartet, the one in A minor. The broadly treated Piano Trio in B-flat Major in the performance by Thibaud, Casals, and Cortot is already famous in the record literature. The stormy, extremely difficult *Wayfarer's Fantasy*—Schubert himself is supposed to have given up the attempt to perform it, saying: Let the devil play this thing!—is masterfully played by Walter Rehberg; also the fullness and softness of the reproduction of the piano sound on the recording proves all prejudices wrong. And Lucie Caffaret forms the variations of the precious B Minor Impromptus into a most vivid plastic.

The orchestral compositions that have been mentioned up to now all belong to Schubert's greatest works. The lighter group of his works is well represented by the entire orchestral portion of the stage music to *Rosamunde,* a "Ro-

samunde Suite," as it were, in a beautiful English performance. That too is Schubert!—the soil of talent, out of
which his (as every) genius had to draw its nourishment.

If it was the composer of songs whom the contemporaries appreciated first, they were following a world-historical
instinct. For here indeed Schubert is the classical composer
of the genre. Classical composers are not usually the founders of an art form—that is the business of the forerun-
ners—rather, they are the ones who bring an art form to its
zenith and, at the same time, frequently at least suggest the
circle of its possibilities; not Michelangelo, but already
Raphael anticipated the Baroque.

Schubert could accomplish the historical deed because
the historical hour had arrived, because, as Goethe would
say, the inheritance needed for every historical achievement
fell to him; the inheritance was this time Goethe's own raising up of the *Lied* to the classical form of German lyric.
Only since the appearance of Goethe's poems in stanzas,
which are in outer form simple like folksongs, in inner form
endlessly varied, has it been decided that both the romantic
form as well as the one influenced by antiquity, that is to say,
that both sonnet and stanza as well as "free rhythms" lie
only on the periphery of the German lyric, although
Goethe himself achieved the highest in both. It is precisely
this form of the strophic repetition, of strophic transforma-
tion that has now become classical, that is suited for Schubert's innermost musical inclination for the variation. Not
the hymns composed without stanzas—however great some

of them are—are the deciding factors of the effect he had, here it is only that he transmits the achievements of the aria to the *Lied;* but it is just those songs that follow the folksong form and yet, through a most intimate interpretation of the poet's word, change them to an entirely new structure that varies from stanza to stanza, and yet musically keeps the strophic unity.

Goethe himself had the right to object jealously to an art that, in courting his own, after all yet only took his most secret wishes out of his words, in order to bury his earthly linguistic corpus and to let his soul rise in the transfigured bodily form of the sounds. On the other hand, however, the whole subsequent development of the relationship between word and tone up to the music drama, felt obliged to these little songs of this composer who in vain pursued operatic success; a most competent witness, Liszt, confirmed this.

Even the *Lieder* had the fate of being really received only (to a small and almost accidental degree) in concert hall and home. The phonograph record unfortunately reflects this fact. Almost everything is there two or three and more times, often published by the same firm, and on the other hand, many of the greatest are missing. Above all, unfortunately, none of the firms, even in this Jubilee Year, dared to publish one of the two great song cycles in a uniform recording. Only a selection of twelve of the twenty-four songs of the *Winterreise* exist; the public's darling, Richard Tauber, sings it.

But still, what singers! Women's voices: The sweet soprano, Lotte Leonard, schooled in old coloratura, who in the trio "The Shepherd on the Rock" (which Schubert for once did not conceive, starting not from the poem but from the singer, really, on commission) vies with the obligatory clarinets; the mezzo-soprano Rosette Anday—how inspired human breath and humming of the wheel are combined in that incredible, lucky throw of the seventeen-year-old's "Gretchen am Spinnrad" [Gretchen at the spinning wheel]; the soulful alto of the mistress of the song, Lula Mysz-Gmeiner—still more precious than in the great antiphonies like the "Erlkönig" [The elf king] or "Der Tod und das Mädchen" [Death and the maiden], in the thoughtful humor of "Der Einsame" [The lonely one]—which was also highly valued by Schubert himself.

The tenors: Soot's voice boldly seizing the dramatic element, Volker's golden radiating one (unfortunately with orchestral accompaniment, which today is quite superfluous with the admirable rendering of the piano tone), Slezak's voice, at fifty, still as youthful as the morning—how he shouts with joy the "Ich schnitt' es gern!" [I'd like to carve it in the bark of every tree!]—accompanied by Manfred Gurlitt, finally Hell's heavenly gentle one, accompanied by none less than Michael Raucheisen. The Baritones: Rehkemper's noble metal—Gurlitt on the piano—and Brodersen's dark abyss. (Since Brodersen died at the beginning of 1926, the recordings are of course technically imperfect.)

Modern people, who hear the grass growing, try, in order to justify their love for Schubert, to pull him out of the bad nineteenth century and to move him into the eighteenth. This is hopeless. His "musicianship" is always "poetically"

bound, thus from a historical perspective, entirely nineteenth century. But for love no one needs to apologize. History after all only tailors the costumes. And the fact that
clothes make people,[1] in history as in life, applies only to
little people. The great ones outgrow them.

The Pre-Beethoven Symphony

Germany's most special and most original contribution to
that pan-European movement, which sought and found the
way back to "nature" out of the Baroque, which had become overly complicated and overly cultured; that movement whose European character we envisage whenever we
mention the name Rousseau, lies in the new music of the
mid-eighteenth century, which Haydn led to victory. And
among the genres it was again the symphony that was most
closely bound up with the social revolution of the new
times. To the symphony, therefore, also belongs that opus,
which then beyond the newly found basis in nature raised a
new peak of the highest culture, which became a lasting
pan-European possession: the Beethoven symphony.

It is from Haydn, not from Mozart, that the path of development starts that leads to the Beethoven symphony.
Mozart, the symphonist, does not stand in this line. If he
had not lived, we would possess the immortal Nine just as
we do possess them. In contrast Haydn traced everywhere in
general and in particular the ground on which Beethoven
then built. The Beethoven audacities have their prototype in
the genius of Haydn's ideas. But what in Haydn arose from
the basic musical originality of this most original of the

great composers and also remained enclosed there, became for Beethoven the vehicle of a spiritual content. One could, for instance, compare just the slow movement of the ninth of the "London" Symphonies, nicknamed "The Clock," with the slow movement of Beethoven's Seventh. Here as there the entire movement is established and ruled by the one simplest possible "time-beating" motif, but in Haydn it is a precious notion of the greatest charm, with which one yet does not perceive the nickname as entirely inadequate; in Beethoven, a direct musical revelation completely removed from the sphere of the possibility of such nicknames.

If Mozart stands outside the line of development, that means in this case simultaneously: above the line of development. Certainly [this is so] in the case of the three symphonies of the summer of 1788. The smile of the E-flat Major Symphony, which glistens through tears; the tragic melancholy of the G Minor Symphony that is present in all the movements, even the minuet; the serene radiance of the C Major Symphony—no jubilation, no power, no ecstasy of Beethoven's symphonic work can rise above it.

By Haydn only the D Minor Symphony no. 101 is available, the one mentioned, one of the less known of his great symphonies, very unjustly unknown; played with tingling vitality and with that transparency that is characteristic of English musicianship, and also very suitable for recording, by the Hallé-Orchestra in Manchester under its conductor, Iren Hamilton Harty. By Mozart there are the three great Symphonies nos. 39, 40, and 41, all played by the Orchestra of the Berlin State Opera under Richard Strauß, so that now the interpretation of Mozart that stresses color over form, by the composer of the *Rosenkavalier*, is preserved for posterity; just the most magnificent of the three, the one in G minor, also in a recent recording, which uses the latest technical advances for the difficult problem of rendering the orchestral fullness; further, also recorded only recently, the Symphony in E-flat Major, played by the London Philharmonic Orchestra under the direction of the other old master of the art of conducting, who still reaches into our times: Felix Weingartner.

Beethoven's Symphonies and the Post-Beethoven Symphonies

Beethoven became the man of destiny for the music of the nineteenth century in general, but in particular for symphonic music. For the symphony—I may remind you of what was said at the beginning of this series of articles—has become this century's central musical genre, the most esteemed by the public and the most sought after by composers. And it was Beethoven who raised it to this level, by filling the public form with also specifically public content, that is to say: political, folk, and cosmopolitan content.

For what is called "cosmic" with the currently fashionable word for Beethoven's orchestral music, that is, plainly put, just that political-cosmopolitan trait. The torn-out dedication page of the work with which the passionate young man threw the banner of his genius over the wall of the fortress to be conquered, the title page of the *Eroica* with the dedication to Napoleon Bonaparte, is not just a biographical anecdote, but a signpost into the heart of his artistic will. It is no coincidence that the connection with a kind of genuine living everyday music can be demonstrated for every great composer—for instance, in Bach it is the connection with the choral; in Haydn, with the folksong; in Mozart, with the dance—for Beethoven, what one always shies away from saying, with—military music. It is in this direction that the marchlike, taut, rousing elements point, that give the stamp to his choice of themes. Not to mention the dramatic introduction, characteristic for him, of entire military-musical themes, as in the *Egmont*—or in the *Leonore*—overtures and in the "Agnus" of the *Missa Solemnis*. The century of the national wars and national revolutions has its musical beginning with the symphonist Beethoven.

The Fourth Symphony [is] the one in which Beethoven leads the language of his two predecessors into the new, his own century, which was now no longer conducted on the podium as a general language, but as a form of expression of the "romantic" in the sense of a fairy tale, which Weber and Mendelssohn then developed further—beside the first who shows his lion's claws quite modestly—the "last romantic" of our days, Hans Pfitzner with the Berlin Philharmonic. The Fifth is available in an English performance—the Royal Philharmonic Orchestra—in which Beethoven brought himself as it were to the tightest formula, conducted magnificently by Weingartner—simple and thrilling at the same time—also technically an extraordinary achievement. Finally, the Ninth, conducted by Fried, with the Orchestra of the

Berlin State Opera and the Kittelchor Solo Quartet: Lotte Leonard, Jenny Sonnenberg, E. Transky, W. Guttmann—

Richard Wagner [1813–83] with his *pro domo* [for my own interests] invented theory of the Ninth Symphony, according to which it is the conclusion of pure orchestral music, was proved wrong by musical history: the symphony is eagerly cultivated throughout the entire century and just in its last decades still has its most significant representatives after Beethoven; yet Wagner's paradox is correct, insofar as the Ninth Symphony anticipates and overshadows the entire subsequent development of the genre. For between the two sidetracks, the romantic symphony, which with Schubert's two symphonic masterpieces branches off from the middle Beethoven and which above all in the Scandinavian North and the Slavic East brings about the group of "national" symphonies, and the symphonic poetic work, which is at least classically legitimized by the *Eroica* and above all by the *Pastoral;* yet the main stem of the development runs to the world-portraying and world-binding symphonic of a Brahms and a Bruckner and finally, of a Mahler. Hans von Bülow's inspired joke, which welcomed Brahms's First Symphony as Beethoven's Tenth, is not actually confirmed by the further development of the Brahmsian symphonic, which grew more and more Brahms-like. But the Brahms-Bruckner antagonism that dominated the musical life of Vienna of the 1880s and 1890s, and that still today runs as a mainline of musical feeling right through Germany, is in its final profundity to be understood only as a modern religious dialogue between the strict-austere-tender North German Protestantism of the one and the South German Catholicism of the other, splendidly extending and returning transfigured. In the wrestling of the disciple of the Catholic mystic Bruckner, in the fight for the symphonic cantata that Gustav Mahler, the Jewish ecstatic, took up again and again, the history of the symphony breaks off, here also entirely under the formal and spiritual spell of Beethoven's last symphonic work. The newest ones renounce—for the present?—"Kettledrums and Trumpets."

I have already discussed the two recordings of Schubert's *Unfinished* under Prüwer and Schillings.

Recently we have also in two recordings a typical representative of what the nineteenth century perceived as a national symphony: [Peter Ilyitch] Tchaikovsky's [1840–93] Fifth. That the Russian aspect in Tschaikovsky is more "coloring" than blood, we sense today after getting to know [Modest] Mussorgsky [1839–81]; in the same way that only [Fyodor] Dostoevsky [1821–81] made it clear to us that [Ivan Sergeevich] Turgenev [1818–83] writes like a Parisian. The performance under Kitschin with the Orchestra of the Berlin Städtische Oper vigorously stresses the Slavic elements of the work that forms a high point in Tschaikovsky's creation; whereas Mengelberg with his Concertgebouw Orchestra intensifies that "European" side through a most delicate agility of his baton and through the fullness of sound and sweetness of his wonderful orchestra, so that one believes in Tchaikovsky's greatness for the duration of listening.

By Bruckner there is the Seventh, conducted by Horenstein, the rising star in conductors' heaven, with the Berlin Philharmonica. True, the work shows Bruckner's strengths and weaknesses—the latter in the outer movements, whose missing inner connections even the most splendid details cannot make a virtue out of necessity; the reference to Schubert does not work, for in Bruckner it is not the Schubertian blissful singing of an idea, but rather an abruptness that is justified in a musical drama by the poetry, which here, however, has the effect of the theatrical, quite in contrast to Bruckner's fundamentally childlike open and pure musical language. The strength comes out as powerfully as ever in the great and compelling slow movement, in the elegy for Richard Wagner—though he was, oddly enough, still alive, and in the grotesque humor of the Scherzo (whose first part, by the way, must be played again after the second, which is not mentioned on the record).

Brahms's First Symphony is played by Klemperer with the Orchestra of the Berlin State Opera. The somber energy of the first movement, the still waters of the middle movements, the dramatic movement of the conclusion—all come out splendidly. The first movement, I think, if my memory of a quarter of a century ago does not deceive me, I have not heard like this even by A. Alan Steinbach [b. 1894].

Catholic Church Music of Two Thousand Years

In the Catholic Church nothing is lost: it preserves the oldest and takes up the newest. Of the Gregorian Chant, this sole remainder of ancient music, essentially faithfully handed down and which remains fully alive, there are three groups of recordings.

The Society for Christian Musical Culture, under the

trademark "*Christschall*" [Christian sound], publishes a series of songs of the Benedictines recorded in Maria Laach, which, with suggestive power, bring you into the space of the romantic church cloisters; "*Grammophon*" offers a series of rehearsals performed very smoothly under the Benedictine and Conservatory Professor R. Pfeffer of the Choral Choir of the State Conservatory of Dortmund, among them a complete high mass; "*Grammophon*" also let the bright, well-trained boys' voices of the Paderborn Domchor sing the ancient tunes in the cathedral itself. Thus the music lover is given the opportunity to familiarize himself with this "most linear" music.

Following this music of Christian antiquity and early Middle Ages, a series of songs by the Munich Cathedral Choir under Berberich, which "*Homocord*" produces, leads then from the sacred folksong of the close of the Middle Ages via the Flemish and via Palestrina and [Orlando di] Lasso [1532–94], to the sacred rococo of [Antonio] Caldara [1670–1736] and into the nineteenth century to Mendelssohn and Bruckner and finally to the contemporaries, a Franz Philipp, a Joseph Haas. As for instance Haas, in his "Wake up" chorus, changes a quite worldly awakening with all his sense of humor into the sacred—one might well think that against such bold ingenuousness a similar opposition would arise, as once when [Saint] Ambrose [bishop of Milan (d.397)] introduced into the church the worldly way of singing of ancient paganism, out of which then the Gregorian Chant arose. At all times it is the sign of the vitality and presence of the spirit that it is not afraid of the world.

Notes
Index

Notes

Foreword

1. For the existential reading of Rosenzweig, see Julius Gutt-mann's treatment of Rosenzweig in *Philosophies of Judaism,* translated from the German and Hebrew by David W. Silverman, with an introduction by R. J. Zwi Werblowsky (New York: Holt, Rinehart and Winston, 1964). For the neo-Hegelian reading see Else-Rahel Freund, *Franz Rosenzweig's Philosophy of Existence,* translated into English from the German revised edition by Steven L. Weinstein and Robert Israel, edited by Paul Mendes-Flohr (Boston and The Hague: Martinus Nijhoff Publishers, 1979). The argument that "Rosenzweig should be read as a philosopher—specifically, a postmodern philosopher" is one of two major themes of Robert Gibbs's *Correlations in Rosenzweig and Levinas* (Princeton: Princeton University Press, 1992), p. 10. Yudit Kornberg Greenberg's *Better than Wine: Love, Poetry, and Prayer in the Thought of Franz Rosenzweig* (Atlanta: Scholars Press, 1996) also claims that Rosenzweig can be, with some modifications, read as a postmodern philosopher (see pp. 129–38). What these positions have in common is that each conflates, in its own way, Rosen-zweig's views of Judaism and philosophy. The existentialist portrait conflates Rosenzweig's commitment to truth and reason with

its own commitment to the rupture of revelation. Conversely, the neo-Hegelian portrait conflates Rosenzweig's view of revelation's rupture with its own arguments about truth and reason. Although the postmodern portrait of Rosenzweig's thought gets past the existential/neo-Hegelian dialectic, it nonetheless succumbs to the same fallacy by conflating Rosenzweig's view of Jewish particularity with a notion of philosophical particularity.

2. See my *Idolatry and Representation: The Philosophy of Franz Rosenzweig (Princeton, N.J.: Princeton Univ. Press, in press)*.

3. Alan Udoff and Barbara Galli, eds. and trans. *Franz Rosenzweig's "The New Thinking"* (Syracuse: Syracuse Univ. Press, 1999), p.98

4. *Ibid.*, pp. 98–99.

5. Hans-Georg Gadamer, *Philosophical Hermeneutics,* trans. David E. Linge (Berkeley and Los Angeles: Univ. of California Press, 1976), p. 9. For a more extended discussion, see Gadamer, *Truth and Method,* 2nd ed., trans. Joel Weinsheimer and Donald G. Marshall (New York: Crossroads, 1989), especially pp. 276–77.

6. Gadamer writes: *"To be historically means that knowledge of oneself can never be complete.* All self-knowledge arises from what is historically pregiven, what with Hegel we call 'substance,' because it underlies all subjective intentions and actions, and hence both prescribes and limits every possibility for understanding any tradition whatsoever in its historical alterity. This almost defines the aim of philosophical hermeneutics: its task is to retrace the path of Hegel's phenomenology of the mind until we discover in it all that is subjective and the substantiality that determines it" (*Truth and Method,* p. 302).

7. Udoff and Galli, *Franz Rosenzweig's "The New Thinking,"* pp. 68–69.

8. *Ibid.*, p. 92.

9. See Rosenzweig's essay, "Apologetic Thinking," in *Der Jude,* Jahrgang 7 (1923), pp. 457–64. Translated in *The Jew: Essays from*

Buber's Journal Der Jude, selected, edited, and introduced by Arthur A. Cohen, translated from the German by Joachim Neugroschel (Tuscaloosa: Univ. of Alabama Press, 1980), pp. 262–72.

10. *Der Stern der Erlösung* (The Hague and Boston: Martinus Nijhoff, 1976), p. 122. Translated from the second edition of 1930 as *The Star of Redemption* by William W. Hallo (New York: Holt, Reinhart, and Winston, 1970, 1971; reprint, Notre Dame, Ind.: Univ. of Notre Dame Press, 1985), p. 110 (page citations are to the reprint edition).

11. The fuller citation is as follows: "Every finite present has its limitation. We define the concept of 'situation' by saying that it represents a standpoint that limits the possibility of vision. Hence essential to the concept of situation is the concept of 'horizon.' The horizon is the range of vision that includes everything that can be seen from a particular vantage point. Applying this to the thinking mind, we speak of narrowness of horizon, of the possible expansion of horizon, of the opening up of new horizons, and so forth" (*Truth and Method,* p. 302). It is not accidental that Rosenzweig does not speak of visual horizon but of a calling and hearing that orients the modern person. Here Rosenzweig is in keeping with his ethically monotheistic, German-Jewish contemporaries and predecessors who privilege sound over vision. For more on this see my *Idolatry and Representation: The Philosophy of Franz Rosenzweig Reconsidered,* chapter 4.

12. Gadamer, *Philosophical Hermeneutics,* p.9.

13. As ramified by his effort at translating the Hebrew Bible into German, with Martin Buber, as well as his continued effort at adult education, Rosenzweig was deeply aware of the particular hermeneutical problem of the modern person alienated from the world of religious tradition. For more on the connections between Rosenzweig's hermeneutic concerns in his densely philosophical writings and in his more popular efforts at adult education and at translating the Hebrew Bible into German, see

my *Idolatry and Representation: The Philosophy of Franz Rosenzweig Reconsidered,* chapters 3, 4, and 7.

1. Introduction: Translating Is a Mode of Holiness

1. George Steiner, *Real Presences* (Chicago: Univ. of Chicago Press, 1989); in *The Defeat of the Mind,* trans. Judith Friedlander (New York: Columbia Univ. Press, 1995; originally published as *La Défaite de la Pensée,* (Paris: Éditions Gallimard, 1987), Alain Finkielkraut examines the history, definitions, and implications of reason, nationhood, pluralism, culture, and philosophy of decolonization. He seeks a respect for reason, as Rosenzweig does, as I argue elsewhere (*The New Thinking,* trans. and ed. by Alan Udoff and Barbara E. Galli [Syracuse, N.Y.: Syracuse Univ. Press, 1998]) and a reassessment of our lost Enlightenment enterprise. Gillian Rose, who, like Rosenzweig, died in her forties, also argues for reason in her remarkable *Mourning Becomes the Law: Philosophy and Representation* (Cambridge: Cambridge Univ. Press, 1996) and that the rejection of metaphysics from ethics in modern philosophy has resulted in the despair of postmodernism. In her introduction she writes, and I quote at length, to give a taste of her lead-crystal clarity, sharp edges and brilliance:

> If libertarianism, with 'ironism' as one version, and cultural pluralism, with its new claimants for 'empowerment', may be dubbed 'post-modernism', then I describe 'post-modernism' as *despairing rationalism without reason.* Far from devastating and discarding rationality, each standpoint aims to redefine it, for otherwise no argument could be devised, no analysis could be conducted, and no conclusion could be urged. Yet, by disqualifying universal notions of justice, freedom, and the good, for being inveterately 'metaphysical', for colonising and suppressing their others with the violence

consequent on the chimera of correspondence, 'post-modernism' has no imagination for its own implied ground in justice, freedom and the good. This ground is therefore held in a transcendence far off the ground, where, with a mixture of naivety and cynicism, without reason and despair, post-modernism leaves analysed and unanalysed according to its tenets the pre-conditions and rampant consequences of power, domination and authority. 'Despairing rationalism without reason' is, I claim, the story of post-modernism. It is the story of what happens when 'metaphysics' is barred from ethics.

2. Steiner, *Real Presences,* pp. 3–4.
3. Ibid., p. 93.
4. Ibid., pp. 112–13.
5. Ibid., p. 58.
6. Ibid., p. 146.
7. Ibid., p. 157.
8. Ibid., p. 157.
9. Ibid., p. 161.
10. Ibid., p. 162.
11. Ibid., p. 163.
12. Besides the untranslated pieces in Rosenzweig's *Der Mensch und Sein Werk, Gesammelte Schriften III, Zweistromland: Kleinere Schriften zu Glauben und Denken,* ed. Reinhold and Annemarie Mayer (Dordrecht: Martinus Nijhoff, 1984). there is the well-known little book, *On Jewish Learning,* ed. Nahum N. Glatzer (New York: Schocken, 1955).
13. Honoré de Balzac, *Lost Illusions,* trans. Kathleen Raine (New York: Modern Library, 1967) One passage reads:

"Blondet is right," said Claude Vignon.
"Journalism, instead of being a priestly order, became first a

party weapon, and then a money-making business. Like all business enterprises, it knows neither laws nor good faith. Every newspaper is, just as Blondet says, a shop where words are sold to the public, of whatever colour they like. If there was a paper for hunchbacks, it would prove morning and evening the beauty, the privilege, and the necessity of humps. A newspaper no longer exists in order to enlighten but to flatter opinions. And so all newspapers will become, in due course, unscrupulous, hypocritical, shameless and treacherous; they will kill ideas, systems and men, and thrive by doing so. All the resources of intelligence will be at their disposal. Evil will be done, and yet no one will be responsible. I—Vignon; you, Lousteau; you, Blondet; you, Finot—will be so many Aristides, Platos, and Catos—men after Plutarch's own heart; we shall all be innocent, we shall be able to wash our hands of all the infamy. Napoleon gave the reason of this moral phenomenon—or immoral phenomenon, if you prefer it—in a brilliant epigram suggested to him by his study of the Convention: 'No one is responsible for collective crimes.' A newspaper may permit itself the most atrocious behaviour; but no one feels that any personal blame attaches to himself" (p. 326).

14. Steiner, *Real Presences,* p. 216, and 6.

15. In *Franz Rosenzweig: His Life and Thought,* presented by Nahum N. Glatzer (New York: Schocken Books, 1961), p. 160. The German is: "Die Leute, die die Bibel geschrieben haben, haben ja anscheinend von Gott ähnlich gedacht wie Kafka. Ich habe noch nie ein Buch gelesen, das mich so stark an die Bibel erinnert hat wie sein Roman 'Das Schloß'. Den zu lesen ist deshalb auch kein Vergnügen" (Franz Rosenzweig, *Der Mensch und sein Werk, Gesammelte Schriften,* I, *Briefe und Tagebücher,* 2. Band

1918–1929 herausgegeben von Rachel Rosenzweig und Edith Rosenzweig-Scheinmann, unter Mitwirkung von Bernhard Casper [The Hague: Martinus Nijhoff, 1979], p. 1152.).

16. Gershom Scholem, *Walter Benjamin: The Story of a Friendship,* trans. Harry Zohn (Philadelphia: Jewish Publication Society of America, 1981) p. 197.

17. Introduction to *Franz Rosenzweig: His Life and Thought,* p. xxix.

18. Franz Kafka, *Description of a Struggle and The Great Wall of China,* trans. Will and Edwin Muir and Tania and James Stern (London: Secker and Warburg, 1960), p. 77.

19. *Franz Rosenzweig: His Life and Thought,* p. 122. The German is: "ich kann mir nicht helfen: so zehn Zeilen zu übersetzen ist besser angewandte Zeit als die längsten Sachen 'über'." The "two magnificent poems" refer to "Der Tag" and "Seele im Exil." In Franz Rosenzweig, *Der Mensch und sein Werk, Gesammelte Schriften,* I, *Briefe und Tagebücher,* 2. Band *1918–1929,* p. 875.

20. Franz Rosenzweig, *Der Mensch und sein Werk. Gesammelte Schriften,* I, *Briefe und Tagebücher,* 2. Band *1918–1929,* p. 952. The German is: "ich habe es immer gesagt: für meine Übersetzungen komme ich in den Himmel, auf Erden habe ich keinen Lohn zu erwarten."

21. *Franz Rosenzweig: His Life and Thought,* p. 134. The German is: "ich verstehe selber ein Gedicht fast immer erst, wenn ich es übersetzt habe, ein kompromitierendes Geständnis." In *Der Mensch und Sein Werk,* I, *Briefe und Tagebücher,* 2. Band *1918–1929,* p. 982.

22. See Rosenzweig's essay "Die Schrift und Luther" (*Der Mensch und Sein Werk, Gesammelte Schriften,* III, *Zweistromland*), pp.749–72, some of which has been translated into English in *Franz Rosenzweig: His Life and Thought,* pp. 254–61. The essay is

also included in that excellent collection of German essays on translation, *Das Problem des Übersetzens,* ed. Hans Joachim Störig (Stuttgart: Henry Goverts Verlag, 1963).

References to the German text of "Die Schrift und Luther" will be to the Störig edition, as, for purposes of practical ease, will be the references to the German original of Benjamin's "Die Aufgabe des Übersetzers," pp. 182–95.

Benjamin's complete little book of Baudelaire translations is reprinted in Walter Benjamin, *Schriften IV. 1,* unter Mitwirkung von Theodor W. Adorno und Gershom Scholem, herausgegeben von Rolf Tiedemann und Hermann Schweppenhäuser: Charles Baudelaire, *Tableaux parisiens, Deutsche Übertragung mit einem Vorwort über die Aufgabe des Übersetzers* (Frankfurt am Main: Suhrkamp Verlag, 1972), pp. 7–63. Here, that which will not be attended to in this chapter can be enjoyed. Baudelaire's original French on the verso pages face, interlinearly, Benjamin's translations into German. For those who have even a little French and German, the experience of reading Baudelaire's truths will be an experience such as Benjamin describes in his introduction—always beautiful, often painful, yet by way of and out from the pain, these truths are always also spiritually uplifting when, in the reading, we step with Baudelaire into those depths of a soul's unrelenting observations. A sublime rise in our mind occurs, something catches hold, a floating upward like a shimmer takes place in us from a place truly *between* the lines. We sense, we actually know, that "the great motif of integrating many tongues into one true language is at work" (Walter Benjamin, *Illuminations: Essays and Reflections,* edited and with an introduction by Hannah Arendt, trans. Harry Zohn [New York: Schocken Books, 1969], p. 77 ["Denn das große Motiv einer Integration der vielen Sprachen zur einen wahren erfüllt seine Arbeit" (Störig, p. 190)]). The translation wakes us up. Benjamin had written: "The particular beauty of so many of Baudelaire's first lines is: their emergence from the abyss" (*Schriften*, II. 2, p. 657). Rainer Nägele notes in this context a phenomenology of waking up, in Benjamin, in Kafka ("Benjamin's Ground," in *Benjamin's Ground*, p. 35).

In English translation "The Task of the Translator" is found on pages 69–82 in Benjamin, *Illuminations*.

23. Two editions of the Halevi translations were published in Rosenzweig's lifetime, the first contained sixty translated poems, the second ninety-two: *Sechzig Hymnen und Gedichte des Jehuda Halevi, Deutsch, mit einem Nachwort und mit Anmerkungen* (Konstanz: Oskar Wöhrle, 1924); *Jehuda Halevi, Zweiundneunzig Hymnen und Gedichte, Deutsch, mit einem Nachwort und mit Anmerkungen* (Berlin: Lambert Schneider, 1927). Rosenzweig's son, Rafael Rosenzweig, published a third edition, helpfully including the original Hebrew, entitled *Jehuda Halevi: Fünfundneunzig Hymnen und Gedichte, Deutsch und Hebräisch, mit einem Vorwort un mit Anmerkungen* (The Hague: Martinus Nijhoff, a member of Kluwer, 1983). For the afterword, I shall give page references to the 1924 edition, to the 1983 Nijhoff edition, and to the book containing an English translation of Rosenzweig's 1927 edition, Barbara Ellen Galli, *Franz Rosenzweig and Jehuda Halevi: Translating, Translations, and Translators*, foreword by Paul Mendes-Flohr (Montreal: McGill-Queen's University Press, 1995). Thus, here, the 1924 edition, p. 109. Nijhoff edition, p. 3. Galli, p. 171.

24. *Franz Rosenzweig: His Life and Thought*, p. 207. The German is: "Am ehesten würde ich mir noch die Bezeichnung als absoluter Empirismus gefallen lassen müssen." In *Der Mensch und Sein Werk, Gesammelte Schriften*, III, *Zweistromland*, p. 161. The term "absolute empiricism" is suggested by Schelling's philosophy.

25. See Robert Alter's *Necessary Angels: Tradition and Modernity in Kafka, Benjamin, and Scholem* (Cambridge, Mass.: Harvard University Press; Cincinnati: In association with Hebrew Union Col-

lege Press, 1991), whose title alone begins already to tell of Alter's interpretation of these thinkers as mystics.

See Douglas Robinson's *The Translators' Turn* (Baltimore: Johns Hopkins University Press, 1991), especially the section entitled "Romantic Redemption," pp. 88–92, which suggests that romantic translation theory is based on the Kabbalist view that "absolute cosmic correspondence, translating sense-for-sense, word-for-word, even letter-for letter, was essential, or more than essential, crucial (anything less meant doom and destruction)" (88). Both Benjamin and Rosenzweig, to Robinson, are romantics. Robinson identifies three characteristics of mainstream translation theory in the West: dualism, instrumentalism, and perfectionism; and, of course, he fits Benjamin and Rosenzweig into the third. See Louis Kelly, *The True Interpreter: A History of Translation Theory and Practice in the West* (Oxford: Basil Blackwell, 1979), especially pp. 30–31; also at 60: "One of the most difficult problems in the history of translation is this mixture of mysticism, aesthetics and philosophy we find in Heidegger, Walter Benjamin and their colleagues. Part of the difficulty is that some attributes of God, including the fact that he is unknowable, have become those of language: the old distinction between sign and thing developed by instrumental theories of language is rejected, as language transcends man, and to some extent creates him."

At the July 1992 Workshops of the International Center for University Teaching of Jewish Civilization in Jerusalem, in the philosophy section that considered ways of teaching Jehuda Halevi and Franz Rosenzweig, Eliezer Schweid claimed in his presentation that Rosenzweig was unteachable. Schweid argued that, because Rosenzweig is a mystic, those who would understand Rosenzweig must feel themselves to be soulfully akin to him, which is not a learned result from study. Those who do not feel akin, according to Schweid, can never learn, teach, or understand Rosenzweig's thought.

26. See, for example, Nahum N. Glatzer's "The Frankfort Lehrhaus," *Leo Baeck Institute Yearbook* I, (1956): 105–22, especially pp. 109–10, where the observation is made: "But he was simply unable to realize the intellectual limitations of even intelligent, university-trained men and women."

27. *Jehuda Halevi*, 1924 edition, p. 119; Nijhoff edition, p. 17; Galli, p. 184.

28. By "cheek" Rosenzweig means, for one, his concluding remarks in the afterword. He had translated the Halevi poems with Arabic rhyme and meter intact, a feat as great as that of Friedrich Hölderlin (1770–1843) translating Greek meter into German, also something which was said could not be done. Incidentally, Rosenzweig had wanted his *Star of Redemption* to be translated into Hebrew after his death, and specified that it should be done in the way of Hölderlin. The final paragraph of the afterword is this: "If I may express a wish, then it is the double one that the water-gauge established here on this small selection will soon overflow, but that not one of my successors in this region may have again the audacity of laziness to fall behind the measure of sufficiency reached here. The excuse that it 'doesn't work' now no longer is at anyone's disposal" (*Jehuda Halevi*, 1924 edition, p. 119; Nijhoff edition, p. 18; Galli, p. 184).

Other examples of Rosenzweig's "cheek" include his remarks to free renderers who want to "give some help to the unfortunate original. Now poetry is not quite as understandable as prose. Obviously this is because the poet did not quite know how to express himself properly, just as the characteristic distance from life of an Egyptian sculpture means only that the artist could not yet do it quite right. [Rosenzweig's "cheeky" note: Fairness requires us not to conceal that the most important authority in the field of the history of classical antiquity, Eduard Meyer, has uncovered an alternate explanation why melancholy lies upon the faces of the Pharaohs from the centuries of the Middle Kingdom: heavy cares concerning government. So it can be read in his history of antiquity.] . . . But would the Apollo of Belvedere really gain substantially from a cutaway and a stiff collar?" (*Jehuda Halevi*, 1924 edition, p. 108; Nijhoff edition, p. 2; Galli, p. 170).

29. On Rosenzweig's and Buber's linguistic-philosophic choice to translate the Name for God as ICH, DU and ER and in their various case forms, see *Der Mensch und Sein Werk. Gesammelte Schriften*, IV, 2. Band, *Sprachdenken-Die Schrift, Arbeitspapiere zur Verdeutschung der Schrift* (Dordrecht: Martinus Nijhoff, 1984); Everett Fox's note in *Genesis and Exodus: A New English Rendition with Commentary and Notes*, "On the Name of God and Its Translation" (New York: Schocken Books, 1983, 1986 and 1990), pp. xxxv–xxxvi. On Rosenzweig's idea of word repetition in the Bible as cues for understanding biblical narrative, see his essay "Das Formgeheimnis der biblischen Erzählungen" [The secret of the form of the Bible stories], in *Der Mensch und Sein Werk. Gesammelte Schriften*, III, *Zweistromland*, pp. 817–29.

30. This is a primary thrust of Benjamin's "On Language as Such and on the Language of Man," in *Reflections: Essays, Aphorisms, Autobiographical Writings*, ed. Peter Demetz (New York: Schocken Books, 1986), pp. 314–32. The essay first appeared in 1916.

31. Benjamin, *Illuminations*, pp. 70–71; Störig, *Das Problem des Übersetzens*, pp. 183–84.

32. For a close reading of Benjamin's texts on language, a reading that not only covers previous, vaguer understandings of Benjamin's theory, but presents a fresh one, see Rodolphe Gasché's essay, "Saturnine Vision and the Question of Difference:

Reflections on Walter Benjamin's Theory of Language," in *Benjamin's Ground: New Readings of Walter Benjamin,* ed. Rainer Nägele (Detroit: Wayne State Univ. Press, 1988), pp. 83–104. Gasché is the first to focus intensively on Benjamin's concepts of communicability and translatability of language.

33. Gasché, "Saturnine Vision," p. 92.

34. Louis Kelly writes in *The True Interpreter,* p. 3: "Friedrich Hölderlin, seeing individual languages as realizations of 'Pure Language', made of translation a search for the kernels of meaning which composed this basic tongue." Kelly, further, shows that the view that "language is an underlying reality to be sought through the use of speech . . . came from Hölderlin's numinous view of language" (p. 60).

In 1927 Benjamin described plans to Gershom Scholem for an anthology of Humboldt's writings on the philosophy of language. (Gershom Scholem, *Walter Benjamin: The Story of a Friendship* (Philadelphia: Jewish Publication Society, 1981), p. 139.

According to Kelly, Martin Heidegger's view that the essence of language is silence, the silence that is necessary to art and contemplation, derives directly from Humboldt's notion of "pure language."

See Hans Aarsleff's excellent introduction to a recent translation by Peter Heath of Humboldt's *On Language: The Diversity of Human Language-Structure and its Influence on the Mental Development of Mankind* (Cambridge: Cambridge Univ. Press, 1988) for an important reassessment of Humboldt and of his influences that includes an irrefutable argument on the input of Condillac's and Diderot's thought, and a sharp critique of Ernst Cassirer, who started an avalanche of misrepresentations of Humboldt's thought.

35. Benjamin, *Illuminations,* p. 77. Störig, *Das Problem des Übersetzens,* p.190: "Wenn anders es aber eine Sprache der Wahrheit gibt, in welcher die letzten Geheimnisse, um die alles Denken

sich müht, spannungslos und selbst schweigend aufbewahrt sind, so ist diese Sprache der Wahrheit—die wahre Sprache. Und eben diese, in deren Ahnung und Beschreibung die einzige Vollkommenheit liegt, welche der Philosoph sich erhoffen kann, sie is intensiv in den Übersetzungen verborgen. Es gibt keine Muse der Philosophie, es gibt auch keine Muse der Übersetzung. Banausisch aber, wie sentimentale Artisten sie wissen wollen, sind sie nicht. Denn es gibt ein philosophisches Ingenium, dessen eigenstes die Sehnsucht nach jener Sprache ist, welche in der Übersetzung sich bekundet."

36. Stéphane Mosès, "Walter Benjamin and Franz Rosenzweig," *Philosophical Forum* 15, nos. 1–2, (fall-winter 1983–84): 188–205. See especially pp. 197–200.

37. Not everyone speaks, and there are the deaf. But language in terms of communicability and translatability is present for all human souls. If it is the contours, as Rosenzweig would say, or if it is the silence, that is the impossible and therefore the urgent to translate that counts, then, as I certainly do not intend to, I am not excluding those who cannot physically speak or hear.

38. The Western philosophical tradition's discussion of language stems from Plato's dialogue *Cratylus,* where the choices are: essentialist or instrumentalist views of language. With their respective theories of language specifically concerning language growth through translating, Rosenzweig and Benjamin introduce a new perspective, most notably that of time (Rosenzweig) or life (Benjamin), which to Rosenzweig would be the same thing. As is well known, Rosenzweig considered at length notions of experience in philosophical thought. Robert Gibbs, in his *Correlations in Rosenzweig and Levinas* (Princeton: Princeton Univ. Press, 1992), importantly emphasizes that for Rosenzweig, experience of revelation is introduced into philosophy *not* as personal experience but

as an objective theological category (which, however, does not, of course, preclude personal experience). This category is of a linguistic nature, and thus, speech becomes primary. Benjamin does not speak of experience between speakers; he opens with that striking statement that seems to be opposed to dialogical, transforming experience, but that ultimately, I would argue, does affirm it. The translation of the German in *Illuminations* is loose here. The convergence of and divergence between Rosenzweig and Benjamin on this point requires, I think, a separate study. The translation is: "Art . . . posits man's physical and spiritual existence, but in none of its works is it concerned with his response. No poem is intended for the reader, no picture for the beholder, no symphony for the listener" (p. 69). The German is: "So setzt . . . die Kunst selbst dessen leibliches und geistiges Wesen voraus—seine Aufmerksamkeit aber in keinem ihrer Werke. Denn kein Gedicht gilt dem Leser, kein Bild dem Beschauer, keine Symphonie der Hörerschaft" (Störig, *Das Problem des Übersetzens*, p. 182).

39. Scholem, *Story of a Friendship*, p. 100.

40. Ibid., p. 121.

41. It was at least two months after the completion of "The Task of the Translator," that is, in July 1921, when Benjamin wrote to Scholem from Heidelberg saying that because he had a pleasant desk there that enticed him to work, he might be writing to ask for Rosenzweig's *Star of Redemption,* which had come out at the end of 1920 and about which Scholem had apprised Benjamin. *Ibid.,* pp. 101–2.

42. Journals such as *Der Jude* and *Die Kreatur* were particularly devoted to such linguistic concerns.

43. "One might, for example, speak of an unforgettable life or moment even if all men had forgotten it. If the nature of such a

life or moment required that it be unforgotten, that predicate would not imply a falsehood but merely a claim not fulfilled by men, and probably also a reference to a realm in which it *is* fulfilled: God's remembrance" (Benjamin, *Illuminations,* p. 70).

The German is: "So dürfte von einem unvergeßlichen Leben oder Augenblick gesprochen werden, auch wenn alle Menschen sie vergessen hätten. Wenn nämlich deren Wesen es forderte, nicht vergessen zu werden, so würde jenes Prädikat nichts Falsches, sondern nur eine Forderung, der Menschen nicht entsprechen, und zugleich auch wohl een Verweis auf ein Bereich enthalten, in dem ihr entsprochen wäre: auf ein Gedenken Gottes" (Störig, *Das Problem des Übersetzens,* p. 183).

44. Steven T. Katz characterizes the Holocaust as a "phenomenological and historical *novum.*" He is the influence for my use of these terms, and I assume that shortly Katz's terms will enter the common language of Holocaust studies. For a brief outline of his enormous work, both in scope and in extent of research, see his very fine lecture, "The Holocaust and Comparative History," which he presented as the 37th Leo Baeck Memorial Lecture in New York, 1994. The full argument can be read in Volume 1 of Katz's *Holocaust in Historical Context: The Holocaust and Mass Death Before the Modern Age* (New York: Oxford Univ. Press, 1994).

45. Rose, *Mourning Becomes the Law,* pp. 35–36.

46. See Scholem, *Story of a Friendship,* p. 100. Benjamin predicted, on the basis of what he witnessed, many twentieth-century terrors. His "Moscow Diary," for example, is a preview of Marxism and its dangers; in *Reflections,* pp. 97–130.

47. "Selige Genien," in the first stanza of Hölderin's "Hyperions Schickalslied" [Hyperion's song of destiny], set to music by Brahms.

48. Benjamin committed suicide at the French-Spanish border in 1940, despairing about acquiring an exit visa and horrified at

any possibility of being deported to a camp. The morning after the suicide, the visa was produced.

49. Finkielkraut, *Defeat of the Mind,* see pp. 114–15, 117.

50. Franz Kafka, *I Am a Memory Come Alive,* ed. Nahum N. Glatzer (New York: Schocken Books, 1974), p. 77.

51. Benjamin, *Reflections,* p. 331.

52. Robert Musil, *The Man Without Qualities,* vol. 3 *Into the Millennium (The Criminals),* trans. Eithne Wilkins and Ernst Kaiser (London: Secker & Warburg, 1960), p. 96.

53. Burton Pike, *Robert Musil: An Introduction to His Work* (Ithaca, N.Y.: Corness Univ. Press, 1961; reprint, Port Washington, N.Y.: Kennikat Press, 1972), p. 126 (page citations are to the reprint edition).

54. Frederick Ungar, introduction to *The Last Days of Mankind,* by Karl Kraus, trans. Alexander Gode and Sue Ellen Wright (New York: Frederick Ungar, 1974), pp. xvii–xviii.

55. Karl Kraus, *Beim Wort Genommen* (München: Kösel-Verlag, 1955), p. 245.

56. *Ibid.,* p. 235.

57. Rosenzweig's note on anthropomorphism, in *Zweistromland* (Dordrecht: Martinus Nijhoff, 1984), p. 735.

58. Franz Rosenzweig, *The Star of Redemption,* pp. 198–99. (1930 edition: p. 143)

59. Benjamin, *Illuminations,* p. 50.

60. An excerpted English version of the afterword appears in *Franz Rosenzweig: His Life and Thought,* pp. 252–54.

61. "The life of the originals attains in [translations] to its ever-renewed latest and most abundant flowering" (Benjamin, *Illuminations,* p. 72; Störig, *Das Problem des Übersetzens,* p. 185).

"Translation . . . ultimately serves the purpose of expressing the central reciprocal relationship between languages. . . . Languages are not strangers to one another, but are, a priori and apart from all historical relationships, interrelated in what they want to express" (Benjamin, *Illuminations,* p. 185; Störig, *Das Problem des Übersetzens,* p. 185).

"[A]ll suprahistorical kinship of languages rests in the intention underlying each language as a whole—an intention, however, which no single language can attain by itself but which is realized only by the totality of their intentions supplementing each other: pure language" (Benjamin, *Illuminations,* p. 74; Störig, *Das Problem des Übersetzens,* p. 187).

"If the foreign voice has something to say, then the language must afterwards appear different from before. This result is the criterion of the translator's conscientiously carried out achievement. It is not at all possible that a language into which Shakespeare or Isaiah or Dante has really spoken would remain untouched thereby. It will experience a renewal, just as if a new speaker had stood up within the language itself. But still more. For indeed the foreign poet calls into the new language not merely what he himself has to say, but rather he brings along with it the heritage of the whole language-spirit of his language to the new language, so that here a renewal of the language occurs not merely through the foreign person, but rather through the foreign language-spirit itself" Rosenzweig, afterword to *Jehuda Halevi,* Nijhoff edition (*Vorwort*), p. 3.

62. Feminist languages are a case in point, for both men and women.

63. Letter to Rudolf Ehrenberg, 1 Oct. 1917, Rosenzweig, *Der Mensch und Sein Werk. Gesammelte Schriften,* I, *Briefe und Tagebücher,* 1. Band *1900–1918,* pp. 460–61. The German is: "Das Übersetzen ist überhaupt das eigentliche Ziel des Geistes; erst wenn etwas übersetzt ist, ist es wirklich *laut* geworden, nicht mehr aus der Welt zu schaffen. Erst in der Septuaginta ist die Offenbarung ganz heimisch in der Welt geworden, und solange

Homer noch nicht lateinisch sprach, war er noch keine Tatsache. Entsprechend auch das Übersetzen von Mensch zu Mensch."

64. Benjamin, *Illuminations*, p. 73; Störig, *Das Problem des Übersetzens*, p. 186.

65. Benjamin, *Illuminations*, p. 73; Störig, *Das Problem des Übersetzens*, p. 186.

66. *Illuminations*, pp. 75; Störig, *Das Problem des Übersetzens*, p. 187.

67. *Franz Rosenzweig: His Life and Thought*, p. 255; Störig, *Das Problem des Übersetzens*, p. 221.

68. Benjamin, *Illuminations*, p. 74; Störig, *Das Problem des Übersetzens*, p. 187.

69. Rosenzweig, *Jehuda Halevi*, 1924 edition, p. 109. Nijhoff edition, p. 3. Rosenzweig repeats his statement that there is only one language in his essay "Die Schrift und Luther," and makes reference to his afterword: "Es gibt nur Eine Sprache—mit diesem Paradox habe ich in einer andern Behandlung des Übersetzungsproblems einmal die Aufgabe, Ziel wie Weg, zu fassen gesucht" (Störig, *Das Problem des Übersetzens*, p. 244).

70. Benjamin, *Illuminations*, p. 80; Störig, *Das Problem des Übersetzens*, p. 193.

71. Rosenzweig, *Jehuda Halevi*, 1924 edition, p. 109. Nijhoff edition, p. 3.

72. Benjamin, *Illuminations*, p. 75; Störig, *Das Problem des Übersetzens*, p. 188.

73. Benjamin, *Illuminations*, p. 82; Störig, *Das Problem des Übersetzens*, p. 195.

74. Rosenzweig, *Jehuda Halevi*, 1924 edition, pp. 110–11; Nijhoff edition, p. 5.

75. Benjamin, *Illuminations*, p. 79; Störig, *Das Problem des Übersetzens*, p. 192.

76. *Jehuda Halevi*, Nijhoff edition, pp. 1, 3.

77. Benjamin, *Illuminations,* p. 82; Störig, *Das Problem des Über-setzens,* pp. 194–95.

78. "'Der Ewige': Mendelssohn und der Gottesname," in Rosenzweig, *Der Mensch und Sein Werk. Gesammette Schriften,* III, *Zweistromland,* p. 815.

79. Northrop Frye, *Anatomy of Criticism* (Princeton: Princeton Univ. Press, 1957).

80. See Harry Zohn's introduction to his translation of Karl Kraus, *Half-Truths and One-and-a-Half-Truths* (Manchester: Carcanet Press, 1986), p. 22.

81. In Frederick Ungar's introduction to *The Last Days of Mankind,* p. xviii.

82. Robert Musil, *The Man Without Qualities,* vol. 2, *The Like of It Now Happens* (London: Secker and Warburg, 1954), pp. 335–36.

2. Rosenzweig's Music Reviews

1. "The Sirens" appears in German and English in Franz Kafka, *Parables and Pardoxes* (New York: Schocken, 1958), p. 93.

2. Peter Kivy, *Authenticities: Philosophical Reflections on Musical Performance* (Ithaca: Cornell Univ. Press, 1995). Page references to Kivy's work, unless otherwise indicated, will be to this volume.

3. In "Rethinking Sound: Music and Radio in Weimar Germany," (in *Music and Performance During the Weimar Republic,* ed. Bryan Gilliam Cambridge Studies in Performance Practice, vol. 3 (Cambridge: Cambridge Univ. Press, 1994), pp. 13–36).

4. Ibid., p. 36.

5. Original German in *Der Mensch und Sein Werk, I, Briefe und Tagebücher 2. Band 1918–1929,* p. 1152; translation taken from *Franz Rosenzweig: His Life and Thought,* p. 160.

6. See *Plato's Phaedrus,* translated with introduction and commentary by R. Hackforth (Cambridge: Cambridge Univ. Press,

1952), especially "The Soul's Recollection of Ideal Beauty," pp. 92–95.

7. The question of suffering usually heightens in intensity and authenticity when it is not posed in a cool academic setting, as for instance as a topic "covered" in the Western tradition of the philosophy of religion: the question of evil, theodicy. Concerns with catastrophe and disaster ran high during and after World War I. Voltaire, with others of the Enlightenment, was focusing on the Lisbon earthquake of 1 November 1755. Walter Benjamin, who returns to this focus in his concern with catastrophe, met his own catastrophe at the early edges of World War II. Walter Benjamin and Rosenzweig, in many regards kindred, were concerned with castastrophe far from university settings. For a discussion of philosophical views of castastrophe, with special reference to Walter Benjamin, see Jeffrey Mehlman, *Walter Benjamin for Children: An Essay on His Radio Years* (Chicago: Univ. of Chicago Press, 1993), 27–32. What can concern us, and only inceptions of which concerned Rosenzweig and Benjamin, is the Holocaust.

8. Remove the anaesthesia and the same pain is felt unless something else occurs during the period of anaesthetization—a natural healing process that simply required bodily time, a surgical operation, a prayer, a new way of viewing things on the part of the sufferer.

9. The note to the poem, "Looking Upward," reads:

People have often asked why the Jewish people have persisted through all despair; and many more or less clever, therefore more or less stupid answers have been given. This poem can teach the true reason which disallows any plural 'reasons.' It begins with the cry out of the abyss of despair, which is so deep that the one called, only cried to to start with—can be cried to, called into question, charged with allegations. And in this cry of doubt and of blasphemy, which exceeds all biblical models, because they are approached by the poisonous juices of a doubting and blasphemous philosophy,—still almost in this cry itself the eye recognizes in the one cried to the one around whom the stars circle; and the mouth acknowedges, breathing freely the might of the one who commands the hosts of heaven; and the heart sinks down enchanted into the view of the divine glory—and has forgotten all despair. (in Galli, *Franz Rosenzweigh and Jehuda Halevi: Translating, Translations, and Translators,* pp. 245–46)

10. See Rosenzweig, *The Star of Redemption,* pp. 251–53. Psalm 115, verses 3–8: Our God is in the heavens; he does whatever he pleases. Their idols are silver and gold, the work of men's hands. They have mouths, but do not speak; eyes, but do not see. They have ears, but do not hear; noses, but do not smell. They have hands, but do not feel; feet, but do not walk; and they do not make a sound in their throat. Those who make them are like them; so are all who trust in them (*New Oxford Annotated Bible with the Apocrypha,* 1977).

11. Rosenzweig, *Star of Redemption,* 252.

12. Ibid., 253.

13. The *Star,* of course, opens with this critique of traditional philosophy, the old thinking. Within this critique, too, there is contained a critique of the denial of time, which entails also the denial of the permission to await answers from another.

14. The notes for this lecture series, "Glauben und Wissen," were published for the first time in the 1984 edition of Rosenzweig, *Der Mensch und Sein Werk, Gesammelte Schriften,* III, *Zweistromland,* 581–95. An English translation is offered in Franz Rosenzweig, *God, Man, and the World: Lectures and Essays,* edited

and translated from the German and Barbara E. Galli, with a fore-word by Michael Oppenheim (Syracuse, NY: Syracuse Univ. Press, 1998), pp. 91–122.

15. *Star,* 372.

16. Ibid.

17. Rosenzweig, *God, Man, and the World,* p. 111.

18. Ibid., p. 120. The "ideals . . . are always clean, because they never come into contact with life." The ideals stand *opposite* life. Traditional philosophy versus faith. Heaven, however, a divine creation, is "on life's *side,* and on that account it looks so much less cleanly washed than the ideals" (121).

3. Franz Rosenzweig: A Commemorative Writing

1. Rosenzweig considered Viktor von Weizsäcker to be a fellow new thinker. He was a member of the Patmos Circle (1914–23) and an editor of the circle's journal *Die Kreatur.* He taught neurology at Heidelberg and Breslau; and, by means of both depth psychology and psychoanalysis, he initiated an anthropological medicine with the goal of curing diseases that are psychosomatically caused.

This short tribute seemed an appropriate introduction to these particular lesser-known writings by Rosenzweig, themselves disclosers and keepers of eternal bridges.

4. Hic et Ubique! A Word to Readers and Other People

1. The original German A. W. von Schlegel translation is "Hic et ubique? Wechseln wir die Stelle.—" The translation of this German translation would be "Let us shift our ground." Shakespeare's original, however, is "Hic et ubique? then we'll shift our ground."

2. *Hamlet,* 1.2: "The funeral baked meats [of peace] did coldly furnish forth the marriage tables [of death]."

3. This is a direct reference to the following quotation from Lessing's *Nathan der Weise*: "Kein Mensch muß müssen und ein Dervish müßte."

4. A German proverb: "Handwerk hat einen goldenen Boden" [Craftsmanship has a golden foundation].

5. For the German word *Geist* occurs in various forms in the following several paragraphs. It will be translated as mind, spirit, intellect, and so on as the English demands.

6. There is a hidden quotation of Friedrich Schiller here, from the first three lines of *Die Bürgschaft* (*The Surety*) (1798):

> Zu Dionys, dem Tyrannen, schlich
> Damon, den Dolch im Gewande;
> Ihn schlugen die Häscher in Bande.

> Damon, with his dagger in his cloak,
> crept up to Dionysus, the tyrant;
> the myrmidons put him in fetters.

5. "Fighters"

1. Hans Ehrenberg (1893–1958), Rosenzweig's cousin who earned his Doctor of Philosophy at Heidelberg, was baptized in 1911 and ordained as a priest in 1925.

7. Lessing's Nathan

1. The reference is from Dilthey's *Das Erlebnis und die Dichtung: Lessing, Goethe, Novalis, Hölderlin* (Leipzig: B. G. Teubner) 1922.

2. Lessing likely based Sittah, a character in *Nathan,* on Reim-arus's daughter, Elise.

3. Reference to the great *Encyclopédié* that Diderot and d'Alembert worked on from 1752 to 1772, attempting to further the age of reason.

9. Stefan George

1. The inquiry read as follows: "On the 12th of July Stefan George will celebrate his sixtieth birthday. Whatever one's atti-tude to the works of this poet may be, his intellectual conse-quence and his great, firmly defined position, force anyone who works intellectually to a decisive position. This occasion seems to us like none other to justify and demand a comprehensive plebiscite among those who are intellectually creative in Germany.

We ask you to participate in this plebiscite through a short autobiographical note in which you depict which role Stefan George plays in your inner development. We will publish expres-sions of any kind, positive and negative."

10. The Concert Hall on the Phonograph Record

1. This is a reference to the story by Gottfried Keller, "Kleider Machen Leute" [Clothes make people].

Index